OMG! I CAN EAT THAT?

Indulgent food minus the boombah

OMG! I CAN EAT THAT?

- - - - - - - - - - -

Indulgent food minus the boombah

Jane Kennedy

hardie grant books
MELBOURNE · LONDON

Published in 2010 by Hardie Grant Books

Hardie Grant Books (Australia)
85 High Street
Prahran, Victoria 3181
www.hardiegrant.com.au

Hardie Grant Books (UK)
Second Floor, North Suite
Dudley House
Southampton Street
London WC2E 7HF
www.hardiegrant.co.uk

Design and Typesetting: Trisha Garner
Photographer: Mark Roper
Props stylist: Leesa O'Reilly
Food stylist: Deborah Kaloper
Food preparation: Michele Curtis, Andrea Geisler

The publisher would like to thank the following for their generosity in
supplying props for the book: Space Furniture, Dinosaur Designs,
Izzi and Popo, The Junk Company, Market Import, Hub Furniture,
Manon, Country Road, Flowers by Joost and The Essential Ingredient.

Cataloguing-in-Publication data is available from the National Library
of Australia.

ISBN 978 1 74066 9 924

Colour reproduction by Splitting Image Colour Studio
Printed and bound in China by C & C Offset Printing Co. LTD

To Mum, Dad and Carrie, all that eating I did as a child had a sense of purpose after all! Thank you for sharing all those dishes with me.

To Rob, Mia, Josh, Max, Bailey and Andy. Thank you for all your dipping, stirring, tasting (and spilling) in my test kitchen. I still love our circus.

CONTENTS

BOOMBAH – (adj)
Word to describe food
that makes your
arse huge.

Introduction

I love food. And I love eating food, but I can't eat whatever I want because I get FAT.

And here's a confession: I love food like lasagne and moussaka and pizza and fried rice. Food we generally refer to as COMFORT FOOD. But it sure doesn't love me. And it seems to have it in for my arse. But do without it forever? Um, is there an option B? I think there is.

When I started on this 'mission', one important realisation came early: comfort food has been hijacked. Our notion of what comfort food is has changed and it's making us HUGE. What used to be an occasional treat has become a super-sized everyday indulgence. It's become DISCOMFORT food. The minute you've eaten it you feel guilty, bloated, miserable and overweight.

In my first book, **Fabulous food minus the boombah**, I wrote about the years of trying every fad diet out there and finally realising I couldn't do white carbohydrates on a regular basis anymore. Rice, pasta, bread, potatoes — they'd make a beeline for my stomach. Some women can get away with it, possibly because they're training for the Olympic games. Some people get there on genes, coffee and cigarettes, or whatever else they're doing. And then there's the rest of us. So I embarked on a quest to create dishes that were basically low in carbohydrates and low in calories but BIG on flavour. Food you can look forward to.

I used the same approach with comfort food. I wanted to find ways to get that hit without the boombah. So I went back to the lab.

After lots of experimenting, I gradually developed versions of all those creamy, cheesy, crispy, crunchy foods we THINK we can't live without.

You'll find there are heaps of recipes with all those comforting elements, but without much boombah in them. In fact not a lot of boombah at all! (I reckon my version of fried rice on page 172 is bloody unbelievable.)

I guess I'm asking you to weigh it up like this: if you're serious about changing your boombah ways, you can go hard-arsed and eat a lettuce leaf and a carrot stick a day, or you can get 80 per cent of the hit of what your tastebuds enjoy and be SATISIFIED and HAPPY and HEALTHY.

Buying exercise equipment off TV is absolutely ridiculous

Trust Auntie Janie here. Buying equipment off the telly is really, really silly. YOU WILL NOT USE IT.

I know. I've bought it MYSELF. I too was a big fat sucker handing over my credit card details in search of a miracle cure or a quick fix in a delivery box. One of the great selling points about the piece I bought was that it could 'easily store under the bed'. And that's where it stayed. Unopened. Until we moved house.

I know that when I don't exercise I feel lousy. And when I do, I feel pretty good. For me it can simply be a (pacey) 30-minute walk. But exercise alone won't make you thin. You have to be accountable for what goes in your gob as well. Exercise is not an excuse to reward yourself with one of those monster muffins. Add to that a milky 'skinny' latte and congratulations, you've eaten your fourth meal of the day.

You're not seven anymore

After releasing my first cookbook I hit the publicity trail. There were a lot of questions about the recipes. Most were good. Others were like this:

'You know your cauliflower rice recipe? I can't stand cauliflower, what else can I use?'
(Um, rice?)

Or, 'I don't like pumpkin or broccoli or zucchini'. What else can I eat?
(Er, potato?)

And, 'I don't like fish' (yes, but you like it battered).

Here is my answer to those questions:

GROW UP.

It's time to get over the histrionics. It's time to start cooking and tasting and enjoying all sorts of foods you've avoided. Thinking you don't like something just won't cut it. In that world, boombah wins. In a face-off between fragrant spicy roasted pumpkin and a bowl of crispy fried potatoes, it's game over. You know the spuds will win. So get rid of the spuds. You know they're boombah.

Try the spicy roasted pumpkin. It's delicious. Take the time to add flavour to broccoli, or zucchini, or cauliflower with sesame seeds, garlic and olive oil.

You'll really start looking forward to these meals and it won't feel like dieting.

Spooky stuff

You know the olden days when people like our grandparents ate three meals a day? And that was it? Look back at old photos... not a lot of fatty boombahs beaming back at you. Well it doesn't take a medical degree to work it out. Quite simply, people ate to satisfy their hunger and indulged occasionally. We now eat and indulge ALL THE TIME.

We eat whenever, *wherever* we want. We eat standing up in a bar, sitting down on a bus, walking down the street, sitting on a beach. Family mealtimes are rare. We're constantly bombarded with food cues — billboards, magazines, TV, newspapers, radio, food courts and fast food restaurants with their flashy eye-catching colours, continuously sending signals to our brain *suggesting* we need to eat. Except we're NOT HUNGRY.

So why do we crave those sugary, fatty, starchy, crispy combinations if our stomachs aren't grumbling? There's a truckload of writing and research on this but I came across one book that spoke to me. It's by the former head of the US Food and Drug Administration, David Kessler. It's surprisingly simple. He suggests in his book, *The End of Overeating*, that the reason we overeat and why we find dieting near impossible is thanks to this dirty little secret recipe: FAT + SUGAR + SALT. Those three elements combined are so intense, we just can't resist. And that's why we find dieting so hard. Once our brain is sent the 'I want junk' signal, we can't concentrate on anything else.

Kessler suggests we have to REHABILITATE our brains. It's a long bow, but if we *re-train* our brains we're in with a chance. And that's the core of the non-boombah philosophy. Yes, we want food with flavour we can look forward to. But you don't have to add sugar and crappy fats to achieve that. I reckon it's important to use, enjoy and savour good food elements like citrus, spice, herbs and chilli — all flavours with impact, telling our brain 'hey, this tastes GOOD'.

How to live longer (and adopting your new mantra: hara hachi bu)

I discovered a very basic trick along the way. Its simple and it works: STOP WITH THE HUGE SERVING SIZES. No more piling up your plate buffet-style.

I've been banging on about the smaller servings theory for a while now. And I've adopted the practice of not polishing off EVERYTHING on my plate. Little did I know there's a name for this. It's a good news story!

There are plenty of tales about long-lived communities, but here's my favourite: the Okinawans from Japan. And they don't just live longer than anyone else in Japan, they live *better*.

The Okinawans have traditionally kept to eating a low-calorie diet: they practise a form of 'cultural' calorie control known as *hara hachi bu*, which basically means they eat only until they are 80 per cent full. (The opposite of *hara hachi bu* is the feeling at about 4.45 pm on Christmas day.) Their low-calorie, mostly plant-based diet also includes wholegrains, fish, a little meat and eggs.

Okinawan centenarians remain lean and have an average body mass index (BMI) of less than 23. Being physical is part of their everyday lives and includes Tai Chi, walking and gardening.

I'm sure there's a killjoy out there waiting to prove it's due to something else but it makes sense to me. Eating proper portions of non-boombah food combined with staying lean and fit seems like the right lifestyle choice.

What to have in your pantry and fridge

I love quoting Dr Phil when he says, 'remove temptation'. DO it. Chuck out anything or everything you know is bad. No one's a saint. So remove the bait. Those cheesy corn chips? You were friends once but now it's over. That packet of Tim Tams hidden in the pantry? You know it's there and it knows you know. Remove at once.

Changing the way you eat shouldn't cost a fortune. You can find good, cheap produce everywhere from supermarkets to shopping strips, and weekend farmers' markets to the larger, more traditional markets. The following ingredients are handy to always have on hand and will also help you cook the dishes in this book. Take your time and get to know your market stall holders, grocers and local butchers.

It may look like a long list but it takes about 20 minutes to gather and you're ready to go.

extra virgin olive oil

sesame oil

light soy sauce

wasabi

Worcestershire sauce

balsamic vinegar

jar of horseradish cream

Dijon mustard

seeded mustard

hot English mustard

canned tomatoes and PASSATA (tomato sauce — try organic)

whole-egg mayonnaise

marinated goat's feta cheese

Greek yoghurt

parmesan cheese

free-range eggs

bacon

ham

tomatoes

continental cucumbers

rocket

red and white onions

zucchini

asparagus

snow peas

capsicums

spring onions

lemons

limes

chillies

garlic

ginger

fresh herbs

fresh bay leaves

kaffir lime leaves

pepper

sea salt

Kitchen notes

When I refer to olive oil, I mean extra virgin olive oil. I buy big tins, usually on special, and just keep refilling a large glass bottle with a cork pourer.

Keep everything handy – don't put the oil, pepper, salt, chillies or lemons away. They *must* stay out on your kitchen bench. Salt is always sea salt. Pepper is always freshly ground pepper, unless stated otherwise. Mayonnaise is always good-quality, egg-based mayonnaise. Greek yoghurt is always thick, natural yoghurt.

You'll also need a microplane grater and at least one really good, sharp knife.

Invest in a non-stick frying pan that has food safety approval. I love cooking with a non-stick frying pan but I'd rather not cook with a pan that's susceptible to its surface scraping off into my (or my kids') food. It's generally the cheap pans that don't last and end up being scraped and battered and lose their non-stick magic. There are great ones on the market that you can go from stovetop to oven. It'll last for years!

Here's a couple of excellent books on food and nutrition

Some reading

Here are a couple of excellent books on food and nutrition:

The End of Overeating: Taking control of the Insatiable American Appetite by David Kessler

The Elements of Cooking: Translating the Chef's Craft for Every Kitchen by Michael Ruhlman

In Defense of Food: An Eater's Manifesto by Michael Pollan

On Food and Cooking: The Science and Lore of the Kitchen by Harold McGee

I don't read novels, I read cookbooks. And these are the top five books I've loved reading, not only for the recipes but for the stories of how all these people made food their passion:

Kitchen Confidential: Adventures in the Culinary Underbelly by Anthony Bourdain

How to Eat: The Pleasures and Principles of Good Food by Nigella Lawson

My Vue: Modern French Cookery by Shannon Bennett

A Life in the Kitchen: Recipes and Reminiscences from a Master Chef by Michel Roux Jr.

The Songs of Sapa: Stories and Recipes from Vietnam by Luke Nguyen

SMALL
--- --- ---
THINGS

Living in Melbourne, I'm spoiled for choice with restaurants that have taken tapas-style eating to new levels (and flavours). It's not unusual to find something called 'small dishes' or 'to start' at the head of a menu.

I love this way of eating as it helps emphasise my own mantra of eating small portions. I find that you can have a few bites or tastes of a variety of dishes and feel satisfied. So why save it for when you just go out?

Here are some ideas if you're having friends for dinner, or it's the end of the week and you've got a little time up your sleeve to prepare a few dishes. And you know those wee little bowls and plates you see in homeware stores and think 'Who on earth would buy such small things, they look like they could be part of a child's tea party set?'. Well, start buying them now. Yep, those small dishes are perfect 'plates' for your guests to eat from. And they also stop the urge to load up your plate like you're at a cruise ship buffet.

The following recipes will do for a group of 6 people. Yes, they REALLY WILL.

Zucchini 'chips' with aïoli

The humble zucchini is transformed into light, tasty 'chips'. It feels like you're cheating. Just don't eat the whole tray yourself. (These need to be cooked close to when you're ready to serve.)

2–3 large zucchini
sea salt and freshly ground pepper
pinch of dried chilli flakes
2 tablespoons olive oil

AïOLI
1 tablespoon light mayonnaise
1 tablespoon Greek yoghurt
2 small garlic cloves, crushed
1–2 teaspoons lemon juice

Preheat the oven to 200°C. Line two baking trays with baking paper.

Using a vegetable peeler or one of those super-thin slicers, shave enough thin slices of zucchini to cover the baking trays.

Sprinkle with the sea salt, pepper and chilli flakes and 'flick' over the olive oil.

Bake for about 10–12 minutes, or until they turn a really golden brown. Take out of the oven and let them cool on the baking tray until they feel 'crisp'. Serve with a small bowl of aïoli.

To make the aïoli, combine the ingredients in a small bowl and serve with the zucchini 'chips'.

SERVES 6

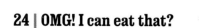

Radishes and anchovy butter

This is so summery, so French and so groovy. Enough said. Don't freak out 'cos it's butter — you only need a dollop on each radish for impact. Oh and get over your 'But I don't like anchovies' whinge. Seriously, anchovies just give food a salty kick. Stop thinking about what they look like!

1 x 29 g tin good-quality anchovies in oil
250 g organic unsalted butter, softened
1 garlic clove, chopped
squeeze of lemon juice
1 bunch radishes

Drain the anchovies and process in a food processor. Add the butter, garlic and lemon juice and process until all the ingredients are well combined.

Wash and trim the radishes and serve with the anchovy butter.

SERVES 6–8

Caesar salad bites

I always have a good cack when I hear people order, 'Just a caesar salad, thanks', thinking they are being 'good' as this is their attempt at eating light. SO WRONG. Caesar salad is dripping in boombahness. But God it tastes so yum. Again, here's a way I reckon you get that caesar hit without the calories.

1 cos lettuce
125 g parmesan cheese
12 thin slices prosciutto

ANCHOVY DRESSING
1 x 29 g tin good-quality anchovies in oil, drained
1 garlic clove
1 tablespoon Greek yoghurt
1 tablespoon light mayonnaise
squeeze of lemon juice
sea salt and freshly ground pepper

Prepare the cos by chopping off the end and the tops of the lettuce. Create about 24 bite-size pieces.

Heat a non-stick frying pan over medium–high heat and add the prosciutto slices. Cook until golden, then leave to cool on paper towel where they will crisp up.

Shave 24 'curls' of parmesan and set aside.

To make the anchovy dressing, place the anchovies and garlic clove in a food processor and process for about 10 seconds. Add the yoghurt, mayonnaise, lemon juice and pepper and process for another 20 seconds, or until smooth.

To serve, lay the cos lettuce pieces on a platter and add the parmesan. Top with a dollop of the dressing, then the crispy shard of prosciutto.

SERVES 6–8

Sesame tuna squares

A combination of sesame seeds gives these nibbles a great crunch and the wasabi mayo gives the tuna a zingy bite.

2 fresh tuna steaks (about 200 g each)
80 g (½ cup) sesame seeds
80 g (½ cup) black sesame seeds
sea salt and freshly ground pepper
2 tablespoons olive oil
lime wedges, to serve

WASABI MAYONNAISE
1 tablespoon light mayonnaise
1 tablespoon Greek yoghurt
wasabi paste, to taste

Cut the tuna into cubes approximately 3 cm x 3 cm. Sprinkle both the sesame seeds on a large plate. Season the tuna squares with sea salt and pepper. Roll the squares in the sesame mix.

Heat the olive oil in a large non-stick frying pan over medium heat. Using tongs, gently place the tuna squares in the pan. Cook on one side for 1½ minutes, then turn and cook for another minute. Do the same on all sides. Place on paper towel.

To make the wasabi mayonnaise, combine all the ingredients in a small bowl.

Sprinkle the tuna squares with sea salt and pepper. Serve with lime wedges and the wasabi mayonnaise.

SERVES 6

Chicken waldorf bites

Yes, the same applies here to the 'I'll just have a salad thanks' fallacy.
See below for the de-fattening of this dish!

12 walnuts, halved
1 baby cos lettuce
250 g skinless chicken breast
1 tablespoon olive oil
1 granny smith apple

DRESSING
2 tablespoons light mayonnaise
2 tablespoons Greek yoghurt
squeeze of lemon juice
sea salt and freshly ground pepper

Preheat the oven to 180°C. Line a baking tray with baking paper.

Place the walnuts on the tray and roast for 10 minutes. Remove from the oven and set aside. When cool, cut in half.

To make the dressing, combine the mayonnaise, yoghurt, lemon juice, sea salt and pepper and set aside.

Prepare the cos by chopping off the end and the tops of the lettuce. Create about 24 bite-size pieces.

Heat a non-stick frying pan over medium heat. Flatten the chicken breast. Add the olive oil to the pan, then cook the chicken for about 5 minutes. Turn and cook for a further 3 minutes, then remove from the pan and set aside.

Just before serving, grate the apple. Chop the chicken into 24 pieces and place a piece to fit in each lettuce cup. Top with the grated apple, a dollop of the dressing and half a walnut.

SERVES 6

Stuffed shiitake mushrooms

I think the texture of cooked shiitake mushroom is absolutely insane…
firm but chewy, smoky and full of flavour. Combined with this tasty pork
filling, these are another ripping canapé.

12 shiitake mushrooms
200 g pork mince
2 spring onions, thinly sliced
2 garlic cloves, finely chopped
½ teaspoon dried chilli flakes
½ teaspoon ground white pepper
½ teaspoon sea salt
1 tablespoon olive oil

DIPPING SAUCE
2 tablespoons light soy sauce or tamari
1 tablespoon sesame oil
1 teaspoon dried chilli flakes
squeeze of lemon juice

Preheat the oven to 200°C. Line a baking tray with baking paper.

Prepare the mushrooms by cutting off the stems and placing them on a tray.

To make the dipping sauce, combine the soy, sesame oil, chilli and lemon juice. Set aside until needed.

In a large bowl, mix the pork mince, spring onions, garlic, chilli, white pepper and sea salt.

Place about 1 teaspoon of the pork mixture in the 'cup' of each mushroom.

Heat the oil in a non-stick frying pan over medium heat. Place each mushroom, filled-side down, in the pan and cook for a few minutes or until the tops turn golden. Turn and cook on the other side for 2 minutes.

Remove the mushrooms from the pan and transfer them to the baking tray. Bake for about 10–12 minutes, or until cooked through. Serve immediately with the dipping sauce.

SERVES 6

Spicy salty seeds

165 g packet seed mix (such as pepitas and
sunflower kernels)

4 tablespoons light soy sauce or tamari

½ teaspoon garlic powder

1 ½ teaspoons sea salt

½ teaspoon cayenne pepper

Preheat the oven to 180°C. Line a baking tray
with baking paper.

Lay the seeds on the tray and roast for about
10 minutes.

Mix the soy sauce with the garlic, sea salt and
cayenne pepper.

Take out of the oven and sprinkle the tamari
mix over the seeds, making sure they are
all coated.

Bake for about 10–12 minutes, or until the
seeds are dark brown (but not burnt!).

Let them cool on the tray, then sprinkle with
a little sea salt and serve.

SERVES 6

Hummus

Ok so I don't do chickpeas, which is a bummer because I love hummus. I know chickpeas are healthy and delicious but the carb count is not on the bonus side for me. But I DO do cauliflower. One day I was mucking around in the kitchen and thought 'what if?'. So here's my version of hummus... boombah-free!

½ **cauliflower**

sea salt and freshly ground pepper

125 ml (½ cup) olive oil

2 tablespoons tahini

1 garlic clove, chopped

juice of 1 lemon

black sesame seeds, for sprinkling

coriander leaves, to garnish

Preheat the oven to 180°C. Line a baking tray with baking paper.

Cut the cauliflower into small florets and place on the tray. Sprinkle with sea salt and pepper and drizzle with some of the olive oil.

Bake for about 30 minutes. Take out of the oven and leave to cool.

In a food processor, add the cauliflower, tahini, garlic, lemon juice and the rest of the olive oil. Process until smooth.

To serve, sprinkle with some black sesame seeds and garnish with a few coriander leaves. This goes well with parmesan crisps (p 55) or some celery and carrot sticks.

SERVES 6

The following soups traditionally shout 'BOOMBAH'. Every time I've seen pumpkin or chowder or French onion soup on a menu or in a cookbook, I've sighed and thought CALORIE ALERT. So I set to making them work for me. And they do!

I've swapped cream for yoghurt or left it out altogether, I've slashed the butter and oil and remember the best-kept secret? SMALLER BOWLS PLEASE.

Roast pumpkin soup with crispy prosciutto

I was SO over pumpkin soup. I thought it was predictable and boring and Lord knows what they put in it at local pubs and cafes… I'm guessing a stack of cream and potatoes to bulk it up. But here's a version that tastes and looks different enough to still be indulgent and taste creamy, with a yum crunch of prosciutto as a treat on top!

2 kg jap or butternut pumpkin, peeled and chopped into cubes

2 garlic cloves, unpeeled

1 tablespoon olive oil

sea salt and freshly ground pepper

1.5 litres salt-reduced chicken or vegetable stock

2 tablespoons Greek yoghurt

1 teaspoon olive oil

4 thin slices prosciutto

Preheat the oven to 200°C. Line a baking tray with baking paper. Place the chopped pumpkin and garlic, in its skin, on the tray. Drizzle with the olive oil and sprinkle with the sea salt and pepper.

Roast for about 30 minutes, or just until the pumpkin changes colour. Remove from the oven and place the pumpkin in a food processor. Squeeze the garlic cloves out of their skin and add to the pumpkin. Process until smooth.

Transfer the pumpkin and garlic purée to a large saucepan. Add the stock and heat through over medium heat until hot. Season with some sea salt and pepper. Keep warm until ready to serve. Just before serving, stir through the yoghurt.

Meanwhile, heat the olive oil in a small non-stick frying pan over medium heat. Add the prosciutto and fry for 1–2 minutes, or until crispy. Keep an eye on the prosciutto as it will smoke a lot. Remove from the pan and drain on paper towel.

Pour the soup into warmed bowls and add the 'stick' of crispy prosciutto to each bowl. Serve immediately.

SERVES 4

French onion soup

What is it about French onion soup? When you really think about it, I reckon it's the combination of the sweet caramelised onion with thyme and gruyère cheese. OK, sorted! Here's my non-boombah version! Yes, it has sweet caramelised onions AND gruyère cheese.

2 teaspoons butter
1 tablespoon olive oil
2 brown onions, thinly sliced
1.5 litres salt-reduced beef stock
2 tablespoons Cognac or brandy
sea salt and freshly ground pepper

GRUYÈRE PARMESAN CRISPS
50 g grated gruyère cheese
50 g grated parmesan cheese

Preheat the oven to 180°C. Line a baking tray with baking paper.

Heat the butter and the olive oil in a heavy-based saucepan over medium heat until quite hot.

Add the onion and stir for about 10 minutes, or until translucent and lightly golden. Add the Cognac and let it 'cook off' for 3 minutes. Add the stock and bring to the boil. Reduce the heat and simmer for about 5 minutes. Season with sea salt and pepper and continue to simmer over very low heat.

To make the gruyère parmesan crisps, place teaspoonfuls of grated gruyère and parmesan cheese on the baking tray, leaving space for spreading. Bake for 6–8 minutes, or until golden and bubbling. Remove from the oven and leave on the baking paper to cool.

To serve, spoon ladlefuls of the onion soup into ramekins or small bowls and top with your gruyère parmesan crisps.

SERVES 4

Chicken soup with carrot, lemon and thyme

This recipe is inspired by one from a cookbook called *Simple Food* I bought years ago at Dean and Deluca when I was living in New York, attempting to further my acting career by going to acting school.

Dean and Deluca was one of the earliest, grooviest (it was right smack in Soho) food concept stores, with aisles of fantastic metal tins filled with herbs and spices with hand-written labels. It was the store for the serious home chef. The truth is, I ended up spending more hours in Dean and Deluca than in acting classes.

Anyway, the original recipe used potato as well, but I've dropped it... trust me, you really don't miss it.

1 teaspoon butter

1 tablespoon olive oil

1 red onion, finely chopped

3 carrots, halved lengthwise and sliced

2 stalks celery, halved lengthwise and sliced

1.5 litres good-quality salt-reduced chicken stock

1 bay leaf

zest of ½ lemon

1 teaspoon dried thyme

300 g cooked chicken, shredded (skinless barbecue chook is ideal for this! Otherwise, slow poached skinless chicken breast)

thyme leaves, to garnish

Heat the butter and olive oil in a large heavy-based saucepan over medium heat. Add the onion, carrots and celery and stir constantly, making sure not to burn the onion. Cook for about 10 minutes, or just until the vegetables turn soft.

Add the stock, bay leaf, lemon zest and thyme and cook for 50 minutes over low heat.

Add the chicken and heat through for about 5 minutes. Remove the bay leaf and lemon zest and serve in hot bowls. Garnish with thyme leaves.

SERVES 4

My chowder

I'm a bit of an aficionado of clam chowder, ever since I ate a bowl on Cannery Row in Monterey, San Francisco. It was bloody good. But bloody fattening. SO I was determined to make this soup work for me.

We don't see clam chowder on our menus much here in Australia, but we should! It's the perfect seafood soup and thanks to my continued love affair with cauliflower, this version tastes so much like the real thing, you'll never go back.

1 tablespoon butter

150 g bacon, finely chopped

1 brown onion, finely chopped

2 celery stalks, finely chopped

2 garlic cloves, finely chopped

sea salt and freshly ground pepper

pinch of cayenne pepper

250 ml (1 cup) clam juice

1 litre (4 cups) salt-reduced fish stock

250 ml (1 cup) skim milk

1 tablespoon agar agar or guam gum (thickener)

2 x 240 g tin clams, drained but liquid kept

1 tablespoon finely chopped flat-leaf parsley

½ tablespoon finely chopped thyme

1 cauliflower, chopped (and cooked in the microwave for 5 minutes on high)

Heat the butter in a large heavy-based saucepan over medium heat. Add the bacon, onion and celery and cook until the veggies are translucent and the bacon is just starting to get crispy.

Add the garlic, sea salt, pepper and cayenne pepper and stir through. Add the clam juice, stock and milk and stir through. Sprinkle over the agar agar and whisk to incorporate. Simmer over low heat for 1 minute.

Add the clams, parsley, thyme, cauliflower and bacon and stir through gently.

Heat again, just at a simmer, until nice and hot. Serve in warmed small bowls.

SERVES 4

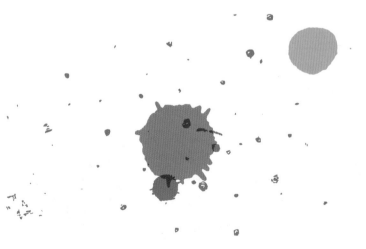

Spicy carrot, cumin and orange soup

I've always loved this combination of carrot and cumin. It's really good. And the orange lifts the soup beyond simple and boring. As usual, I can't help but add some chilli to give the soup more depth.

1 teaspoon butter
1 tablespoon olive oil
1 leek, trimmed and chopped
750 g carrots, chopped
1 small knob of fresh ginger, finely grated
½ teaspoon ground cumin
½ teaspoon dried chilli flakes
juice of 1 orange
zest of ½ orange
1 litre (4 cups) salt-reduced chicken stock
sea salt and freshly ground pepper
chopped coriander, to garnish

Heat the butter and olive oil in a large heavy-based saucepan and add the leeks. Cook for about 3 minutes, stirring the leeks constantly, then add the carrots. Stir again. Add the ginger, cumin and chilli. Stir some more.

Add the orange juice, zest, stock and sea salt and pepper. Reduce the heat and simmer, with the lid on, for about 40 minutes.

Let the soup cool a little, then purée in a food processor. Do in batches if necessary.

Pour the soup back into saucepan and reheat. Add a little water or stock if it's too thick.

Serve in warmed bowls and garnish with some chopped coriander.

SERVES 4

Mushroom soup

Mushroom soup doesn't need to be Boombah. It's a very 'cheffy' touch to place the cooked mushrooms in the bowl before pouring in the soup. You could even serve the soup this way at the table if you really wanted to show off!

1 tablespoon olive oil

600 g chestnut or field mushrooms, thickly sliced

2 teaspoons butter

2 garlic cloves, finely chopped

sea salt and freshly ground pepper

1 litre (4 cups) salt-reduced vegetable stock

2 tablespoons Greek yoghurt

100 g extra chestnut and field mushrooms, finely chopped

1 large handful chopped flat-leaf parsley

PARMESAN CRISPS

125 g grated parmesan cheese

Preheat the oven to 180°C. Line a baking tray with baking paper.

Heat the olive oil in a heavy-based saucepan over medium heat. Add the mushrooms and cook for about 1 minute.

Add 1 teaspoon of the butter, the garlic, and some salt and pepper. Stir for about 10 minutes, or until the mushrooms start to turn a bit golden. Add the stock and simmer for about 20 minutes. Remove the saucepan from the heat and allow to cool slightly.

Pour the soup and the yoghurt into a food processor and process until smooth. You may have to do this in batches. Pour the soup back into the saucepan and keep warm over low heat.

To make the parmesan crisps, place teaspoonfuls of the parmesan cheese on the baking trays, leaving space for spreading. Bake for 6–8 minutes, or until golden and bubbling. Remove from the oven and leave on the baking paper to cool.

Heat 1 teaspoon of the butter and some olive oil in a non-stick frying pan over medium heat. Add the finely chopped mushrooms to the pan and stir constantly for a few minutes. Add the parsley and some sea salt and pepper, to taste. Cook until golden.

To serve, pour the hot soup into a large jug. Place a handful of the cooked mushrooms into the base of four small terrine dishes or bowls. Pour the soup over the mushrooms. Serve with the parmesan crisps.

You could even give each person their own little jug to pour their own serve. So fancy!

SERVES 4

Pho no noodles

One of my go-to lunches when I'm at work is a Thai tom yum or a Vietnamese pho soup. However, I don't do noodles because noodles give me the chumba wumba arse. So I always ask for NO NOODLES PLEASE when I order. This is ALWAYS met with a rather perplexed look from the person behind the counter and I often have to say 'I'll pay the same' or 'I'll pay extra'. And I do. Bizarre but true.

Anyway, Vietnamese pho is a fragrant, elegant soup with subtle flavours and a chilli punch that will fill you up 'til dinner!

400 g scotch fillet steak

1 lemongrass stem, white part only, thinly sliced

2 red chillies, plus extra to garnish

1 large garlic clove

1 small knob fresh ginger

sea salt and freshly ground pepper

1.5 litres (6 cups) salt-reduced beef stock

½ tablespoon fish sauce

3 kaffir lime leaves, shredded

1 bunch baby bok choy, chopped

bean shoots, to garnish

1 bunch Thai basil leaves

1 bunch coriander

lime wedges, to serve

Put the steak in the freezer about 30 minutes before serving. (This will make it easier to slice it thinly).

Place the lemongrass, chilli, garlic and ginger in a mortar and pestle and pound to a paste. Add a pinch of sea salt.

Remove the steak from the freezer and slice thinly. Set aside.

Add the stock to a saucepan over medium heat and bring to the boil. Add the spicy paste, fish sauce and kaffir lime leaves and continue to simmer for about 5 minutes. Add the beef slices one at a time (use tongs), then add the bok choy. Simmer for another 1–2 minutes.

To serve, fill each bowl with a handful of bean shoots, some pieces of the beef, and some bok choy. Pour the 'pho' or broth over the top. Add some Thai basil leaves, coriander, chilli and a wedge of lime.

SERVES 4

PIEMAKINS

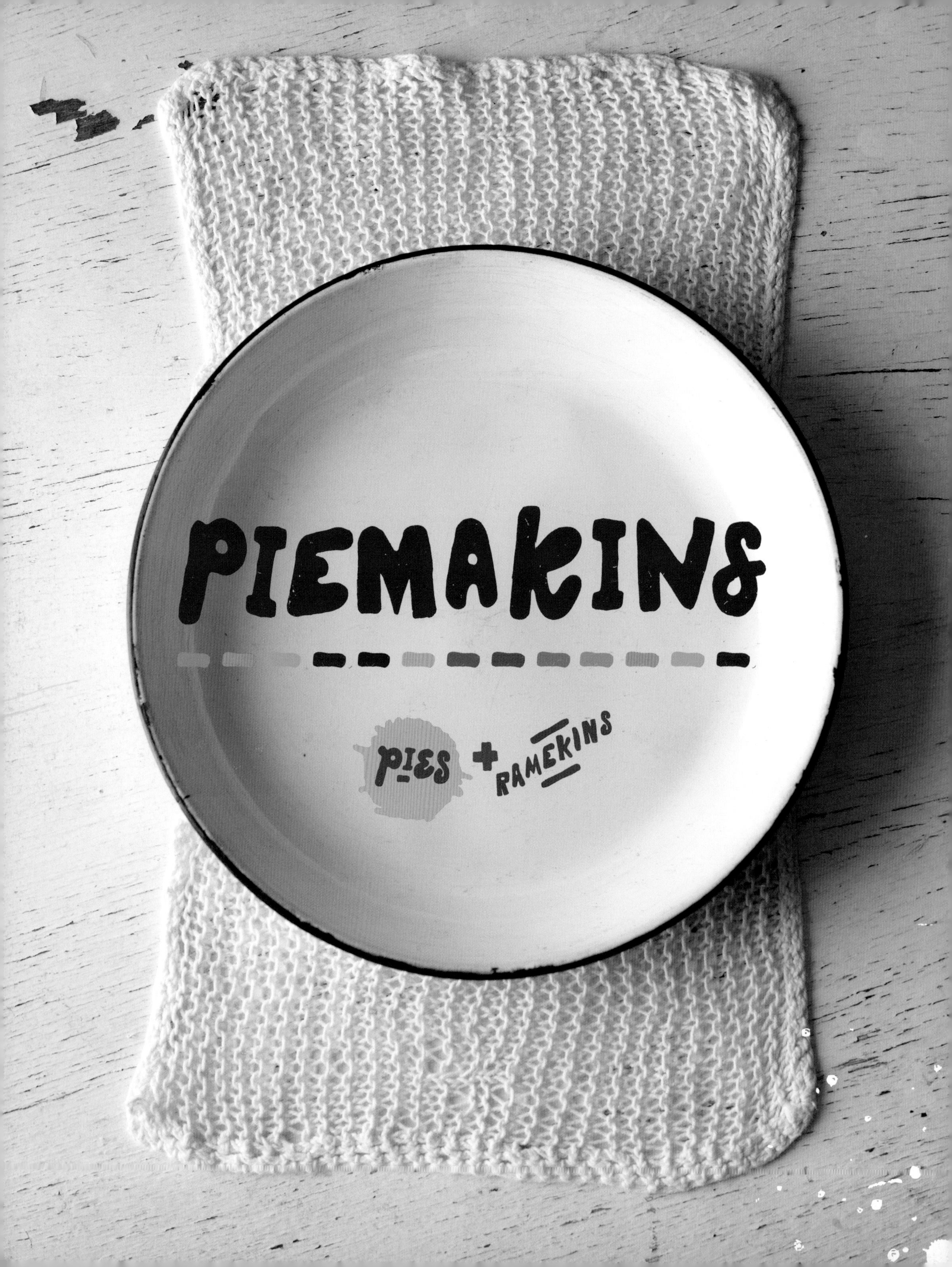

Yep, I love making up new words for dishes (PIE-MA-KINS). These are my version of pies minus the pastry (which is generally the boombah bit). They're served in ramekins, so they're a cross between a ramekin and a pie. Get it?? They're the perfect serving size as far as I'm concerned and give you that special 'comfort' hit, as anything that comes out of the oven bubbling and hot works for me!

Beef and peppercorn piemakin

1 tablespoon olive oil

400 g sirloin or blade steak, cut into cubes

1 teaspoon butter

1 brown onion, halved and sliced

2 garlic cloves, crushed

1 carrot, halved lengthways and chopped

12 button mushrooms, quartered

1 tablespoon green peppercorns, drained

1 sprig thyme, finely chopped

1 sprig rosemary, finely chopped

1 bay leaf

4 tablespoons red wine

300 ml salt-reduced beef stock

125 g parmesan cheese (for crisps, p 55)

Preheat the oven to 180°C. Line a baking tray with baking paper.

Place 4 heaped tablespoons of grated parmesan on the baking paper, to form four circles (this will make the pie 'tops').

Bake for about 8–10 minutes, watching constantly to make sure they don't overbrown. Remove from the oven when the parmesan starts bubbling. Leave to cool on the baking paper until ready to use.

Heat the olive oil in a non-stick frying pan over medium heat. Add the beef, sautéing until it turns slightly brown. Remove the beef with a spoon, including the juices in the pan.

Using the same frying pan, add the butter, then add the onion, garlic and carrot. Cook until the onion just softens, stirring constantly. You may need to add a tablespoon of water to keep it moist.

Add the mushrooms, peppercorns, thyme, rosemary and bay leaf and stir for about 3 minutes. Add the red wine and let it sizzle. Add the meat and juices back to the pan, stir, and then add the stock.

Cover with a lid, turn down the heat and simmer for about 45 minutes. Check from time to time that there is enough liquid. If not, add a little more stock. Remove the lid and cook for another 10 minutes, reducing the sauce a little.

Ladle the mixture into 4 ramekins and top each ramekin with a parmesan crisp (p 55) as the pie lid. Serve with a garden salad.

SERVES 4

Chicken, leek and mushroom piemakin

1 tablespoon olive oil

2 small skinless chicken fillets (about 140 g each), cut into cubes

2 garlic cloves, crushed

2 leeks, finely sliced

12 Swiss brown mushrooms, sliced and cut into quarters

1 sprig thyme

1 sprig rosemary, finely chopped

sea salt and freshly ground pepper

2 tablespoons Greek yoghurt

ZUCCHINI 'CRUST'

1 small zucchini, peeled and grated

1 egg, whisked

50 g (⅓ cup) grated light mozzarella cheese

50 g (½ cup) grated parmesan cheese

Preheat the oven to 180°C. Line a baking tray with baking paper.

To make the zucchini crust, combine the zucchini, egg and mozzarella cheese in a bowl. Spread this mixture onto the baking paper, making four circles in the shape of a pie lid.

Bake for about 20 minutes, or just until the zucchini crust starts to change colour. Remove from the oven and leave on the baking paper to cool.

Heat the olive oil in a non-stick frying pan over medium heat. Cook the chicken for about 5–6 minutes. Remove the chicken with a slotted spoon, leaving the juices in the pan, and set aside.

Add the garlic and leeks to the pan. Sauté for about 5 minutes, stirring constantly and making sure the leeks and garlic don't brown too much. Add the mushrooms, thyme, rosemary, sea salt and pepper and cook for another 6–8 minutes. Stir in the yoghurt.

Divide the mixture between 4 ramekins and top each one with a zucchini 'lid'. Sprinkle with the parmesan cheese and bake for about 10–12 minutes, or until brown and bubbling. Serve immediately.

SERVES 4

Fish piemakin

1 teaspoon butter

1 tablespoon olive oil

1 onion, halved and sliced

1 garlic clove, crushed

4 tablespoons white wine

2 teaspoons wholegrain mustard

½ teaspoon cayenne pepper

sea salt and freshly ground pepper

250 ml (1 cup) salt-reduced fish or vegetables stock

400 g firm white fish fillets, cut into cubes

1 teaspoon lemon juice

zest of ½ lemon

1 small handful tarragon, finely chopped

1 small handful flat-leaf parsley, finely chopped

50 g (½ cup) grated parmesan cheese

CAULIFLOWER TOPPING

1 cauliflower, cut into florets

1 tablespoon milk

1 tablespoon Greek yoghurt

1 teaspooon horseradish

sea salt and freshly ground pepper

Preheat the oven to 180°C. Heat the butter and olive oil in a non-stick frying pan over medium heat. Cook the onion and garlic until softened. Add the wine and let it sizzle.

Stir in the mustard, cayenne pepper and the sea salt and pepper. Add the stock and let it bubble for a few minutes.

Add the fish to the pan with the lemon juice, lemon zest, tarragon and parsley. Turn down the heat to a simmer and cook for about 5 minutes.

To make the cauliflower topping, microwave the cauliflower and milk in a microwave -safe dish for about 5–6 minutes, or until the cauliflower is tender. Add the yoghurt, horseradish and sea salt and pepper and whizz in a food processor until it resembles mashed potato.

Using a slotted spoon, transfer the fish and onion mixture into 4 ramekins. Add a little of the juice to moisten and top with a layer of the cauliflower topping. Sprinkle parmesan cheese on top and bake for about 25 minutes, or until golden.

SERVES 4

Beef, Lamb
& Pork

It's generally the sides and sauces we add to our meat dishes that 'boombahs' them up. Oh, and the ENORMOUS serving sizes. These tasty dishes are easy to prepare and really satisfying, but please stick to the amounts I suggest. For example, a recipe stating 140 grams of meat per person DOES NOT convert to 240 grams, ok?

Lamb tends to be expensive at times so I've stuck with the cheaper cuts here — shanks or shoulder, and pork is lean, tasty and relatively cheap.

Pork cevapcici and mustard pots with rocket, parsley and red onion salad

I love sausages, but there's no secret as to why they're called 'mystery bags'. I prefer to eat my food without the mystery thanks. These are so, so tasty with the spiciness of fennel seeds and a hint of chilli. I feel so confident about these snags that I reckon they could become a staple at your joint.

1 teaspoon fennel seeds
1 teaspoon dried chilli flakes
1 teaspoon sea salt
1 teaspoon black peppercorns
500 g pork mince
1 large onion, finely chopped
1 garlic clove, finely chopped
55 g (½ cup) almond meal
1 tablespoon olive oil

SALAD
1 bunch flat-leaf parsely
1 red onion, halved and finely sliced
100 g rocket leaves
sea salt and freshly ground pepper
olive oil, for drizzling
squeeze of lemon juice

Crush the fennel seeds, chilli, sea salt and peppercorns in a mortar and pestle.

Combine the mince, spices, onion, garlic and almond meal in a large mixing bowl and mix well.

Take a small handful of the mince mixture and shape into 12 small fat 'fingers'. Line up on a plate and refrigerate until ready to cook.

Heat the olive oil in a frying pan over medium–high heat. Add the cevapcici and cook until well cooked through.

To make the salad, combine the parsley leaves and rocket, then toss through the red onion and season. Drizzle with olive oil and a squeeze of lemon juice and serve with the cevapcicis.

SERVES 4

Vietnamese beef with mint and peanuts

3 spring onions, trimmed and chopped

5 garlic cloves, finely chopped

2 lemongrass stems, white part only, finely chopped

4 tablespoons fish sauce

sea salt and freshly ground pepper

450 g beef sirloin or fillet, cut into strips

2 small red chillies, finely chopped

2 teaspoons sugar

squeeze of lime juice

3 tablespoons rice vinegar

1 iceberg lettuce, shredded

2 Lebanese cucumbers, cut into matchsticks

1 carrot, cut into matchsticks

50 g bean sprouts

1 bunch coriander leaves

1 bunch Vietnamese mint leaves

60 g roasted peanuts, coarsely chopped

Combine the spring onions, 3 garlic cloves and the lemongrass in a mortar and pestle and pound to a coarse paste. Add 1 tablespoon of fish sauce and a little sea salt and pepper and stir through. Transfer the marinade to a bowl. Add the beef and marinate for about 1 hour (less will do if you're pushing time).

To make the dressing, combine the remaining garlic and fish sauce, the chilli, sugar, lime juice and vinegar and stir until the sugar dissolves. Set aside.

Thread the beef onto bamboo skewers which have been soaked in water for 10 minutes. Heat a chargrill pan over high heat and cook the beef skewers for 1–2 minutes on each side.

Combine the lettuce, cucumber, carrot, bean sprouts and herbs in a large bowl. Remove the beef from the skewers, add to the bowl, drizzle with dressing and toss to combine. Divide among bowls, scatter with peanuts and serve immediately.

SERVES 4

Corn beef with quick homemade mustard pickle

Polarising, yes. You either love this dish or hate it. I happen to LOVE it! Mum never served her version of corned beef with white parsley sauce, as many of you are familiar with, so I never knew what I was missing out on. I did love the mustard pickles we used to have, but that was from a jar and has a million ingredients and heaps of sugar, so I thought 'why not make my own version of pickles with cauliflower?'.

1 x 500 g piece corned beef

3 bay leaves

10 peppercorns

3 garlic cloves, crushed

1 lemon, halved

1 onion, peeled

8 cloves

MUSTARDY PICKLES

½ cauliflower, cut into florets

2 teaspoons Dijon mustard

½ teaspoon hot English mustard

sea salt dissolved in 30 ml water

1 tablespoon white vinegar

1 teaspoon turmeric

Cover the beef with cold water in a large saucepan. Add the bay leaves, peppercorns, garlic and lemon. Stud the whole peeled onion with the cloves and add to the pan. Bring to the boil, then turn down to a simmer and cook for at least 3 hours.

Take out the beef, slice and serve with steamed carrots, steamed savoy cabbage and mustardy pickles.

To make the mustardy pickles, place the cauliflower in a microwave safe container and cook on high for about 3 minutes (or simply steam in a saucepan). The cauliflower should still be firm to touch.

In a saucepan, add both the mustards, water vinegar and turmeric and heat gently. Add the cauliflower and stir well. Cook for about 10 minutes on a low heat, stirring occasionally. Serve hot or cold.

SERVES 4

Lamb loin dusted with dukkah with parsley and red onion salad

This is a lean, mean tasting dish. Dukkah is spicy, nutty and tasty and continues my obsession with sesame seeds.

2 tablespoons dukkah (available from specialty stores)
2 loins of lamb (about 220 g each)
sea salt and freshly ground pepper
1 tablespoon olive oil
1 large bunch flat-leaf parsley leaves
1 continental cucumber, sliced on the diagonal
1 large red onion, finely sliced
olive oil, for drizzling
juice of 1 lemon
spicy roast pumpkin, to serve (p 179)

Place the dukkah on a plate. Season the lamb with sea salt and pepper and roll in the dukkah.

Heat the olive oil in a non-stick frying pan over medium–high heat. Cook the lamb for about 2–3 minutes on one side, then turn and cook for another 2 minutes. Remove from the pan the set aside to rest.

Combine the parsley, cucumber and red onion. Season with sea salt and pepper, drizzle over the olive oil and add the lemon juice. Toss well.

To serve, slice each loin into thick slices on the diagonal and plate up with some of the salad on the side. Serve with spicy roast pumpkin (p 179) if you like.

SERVES 2

Steak tartare

Before you freak out about eating raw beef, let me tell you once you try this dish you'll be converted. It doesn't taste like you're eating raw anything… just a creamy, velvety spicy texture with the added kick of chilli. And I'm a girl who likes it HOT, so feel free to adjust your chilli/seasonings. And naturally, as the meat is the hero in the dish, please use only the VERY best eye fillet steak you can manage and keep refrigerated until the very moment you're about to use it.

400 g eye fillet steak

1 tablespoon cornichons (little dill pickles), finely chopped

1 red onion, finely chopped

1 tablespoon capers, rinsed and chopped

1 tablespoon chopped flat-leaf parsley

2 teaspoons Dijon mustard

29 g tin good-quality anchovies in oil, drained and chopped (optional)

1 teaspoon Worcestershire sauce

dash of Tabasco

½ teaspoon dried chilli flakes

sea salt and freshly ground pepper

2 egg yolks

lemon wedges, to serve

The best way to cut the beef is by hand with a very sharp knife on a spotlessly clean chopping board.

Chop the meat very finely. (If you whizz it in a food processor it tends to go a bit sloppy.) Transfer to a bowl, cover with plastic wrap and refrigerate until just before serving.

When ready to serve, take the meat out of the fridge and add the cornichons, onion, capers, parsley, mustard, anchovies (if using), Worcestershire sauce, Tabasco, chilli and sea salt and pepper.

To serve, place a mound of tartare in the centre of each plate and make a slight dip in the top of the beef. Add your egg yolk to the middle and a lemon wedge on the side. Serve immediately.

SERVES 4

Osso buco

8 pieces veal osso buco

sea salt and freshly ground pepper

2 tablespoons olive oil

1 teaspoon butter

150 g chopped onion

140 g chopped celery

150 g chopped carrot

2 sprigs rosemary, chopped

1 sprig thyme

1 bay leaf

125 ml (½ cup) white wine

2 x 400 g tins tomatoes

5 garlic cloves, chopped

500 ml (2 cups) salt-reduced beef stock

GREMOLATA

zest of 2 lemons

1 small handful flat-leaf parsley, chopped

2 garlic cloves, freshly chopped

Season the veal with sea salt and pepper. Heat 1 tablespoon of the olive oil and the butter in a large heavy-based casserole dish over medium heat. Add the veal and brown lightly.

Remove from the pan and set aside. In the same pot, add the other tablespoon of oil and sauté the chopped onions until transparent.

Add the celery, carrots, rosemary, thyme and bay leaf and stir. Cook for a few minutes, then add the white wine and stir well.

Place the veal on top of the vegetables, add the tomatoes and garlic and enough stock to cover the meat.

Bring to the boil, then lower the heat to a simmer and add a lid of baking paper cut to size to fit on top of the liquid. This will keep the meat tender and moist. Pop on the lid as well.

Simmer for 45 minutes, then check to make sure there is still plenty of sauce. If not, add a little more stock. Cover and cook for a further 45 minutes.

Remove both lids and simmer for about 15 minutes to help the sauce thicken.

To make the gremolata, combine the lemon zest, parsley and garlic in a bowl.

To serve, ladle the meat and veggies in a warmed bowl and sprinkle generously with the gremolata. Serve with cauliflower rice (p 178).

SERVES 4

Thai beef and pumpkin red curry

2 tablespoons sunflower oil

1 small red chilli, finely chopped

1 garlic clove, crushed

1 small knob of ginger, peeled and finely chopped

1 onion, halved and sliced

500 g diced beef

2 tablespoons red curry paste

3 tablespoons light coconut milk

185 ml (¾ cup) coconut water (from the same can of coconut milk)

2 tablespoons fish sauce

1 teaspoon sugar

1 kg jap or butternut pumpkin, peeled and cubed

4 kaffir lime leaves, shredded

Thai basil leaves, to garnish

Heat the sunflower oil in a large non-stick frying pan over low–medium heat and sauté the chilli, garlic and ginger, being careful not to burn. Add the onion and stir for about 2 minutes.

Turn up the heat, add the beef and cook until slightly brown. Add the curry paste (be careful as it will splatter). Stir to release the flavours and coat the beef.

Add the coconut milk and coconut water, stirring well, then add the fish sauce and sugar. Turn the heat down to a simmer, cover with the lid and cook for about 10 minutes.

Add the pumpkin, stir through and cook for a further 30 minutes, or until the pumpkin is cooked. Stir through the kaffir lime leaves.

Garnish with some Thai basil and serve with cauliflower rice (p 178).

SERVES 4

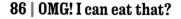

Lamb shanks two ways: Asian spices

Asian lamb shanks? You bet. And again, by cooking the shanks slowly, the meat falls off the bone and the spicy, fragrant mix is a brilliant treat. Get out your spice kit for this one. This recipe was inspired by the fabulous Kylie Kwong. Thank you Kylie!

LAMB SHANKS WITH ASIAN SPICES

2 teaspoons fennel seeds

10 cardamom pods

½ teaspoon ground star anise

½ teaspoon cumin seeds

½ teaspoon ground cinnamon

2 red chillies, chopped

3 small garlic cloves, crushed

1 knob of ginger, peeled and crushed

small bunch coriander, leaves and roots chopped

½ teaspoon turmeric

125 ml (½ cup) olive oil

4 lamb shanks, trimmed

sea salt and freshly ground pepper

1 tablespoon olive oil

splash of dry white wine

750 ml (3 cups) salt-reduced chicken stock

juice of 1 lime

Preheat the oven to 180°C. Place the fennel seeds, cardamom pods, star anise, cumin seeds and cinnamon in a small non-stick frying pan. Cook over medium–high for about 1–2 minutes. Make sure you keep stirring.

Transfer the mixture to a mortar and pestle and smash the spices around. After pounding, take out the cardamom husks.

Add the chilli, garlic, ginger and coriander and pound. Add the turmeric, a pinch of sea salt and the olive oil and mix until well combined.

Heat a non-stick frying pan over medium heat and add the spice mix. Cook on low heat for about 5 minutes. Turn off the heat and set aside.

Season the lamb shanks with sea salt and pepper. Heat a large casserole dish on the stovetop, add 1 tablespoon of oil, then add the shanks. Brown on each side. This should take a few minutes. Add your spice mix and coat the shanks well. Add the wine. Take off the heat, cover the shanks with the stock and cover with foil or a lid.

Roast for 1 hour, then take the foil or lid off and roast for another hour. The lamb should fall off the bone.

Transfer to heated bowls, drizzle with lime juice and serve with cauliflower rice (p 178).

SERVES 4

... and with carrot mash

Definitely one of those dishes I can't go past on a menu and as soon as it turns cold, it's a go-to for the weekend. The problem was the whopping serve of buttery, creamy potato mash, and the 4 shanks I could scoff in one sitting. That had to stop. So 1 big shank per person should do the trick.

4 lamb shanks, trimmed
sea salt and freshly ground pepper
1½ tablespoons olive oil
1 onion, diced
2 carrots, chopped and diced
2 celery stalks, chopped and diced
1 leek, cleaned, chopped and diced
2 garlic cloves, finely chopped
1 tablespoon finely chopped rosemary
2–3 sprigs thyme
125 ml (½ cup) red wine
2 cups salt-reduced beef stock
1 x 400 g tin crushed tomatoes
12 peppercorns
1 bay leaf

FOR THE MASH
4 large carrots, chopped
1 garlic clove, finely chopped
pinch of white pepper
pinch of sea salt
1 teaspoon butter
1 tablespoon Greek yoghurt

Preheat the oven to 180°C. Season the shanks with sea salt and pepper.

Heat 1 tablespoon of the olive oil in a large heavy-based saucepan over medium heat. Lightly brown the shanks for 6–8 minutes, turning often. Remove the shanks and set aside.

Add the remaining olive oil and the onion, carrots, celery, leek, half the garlic, and the rosemary and thyme to the pan. Stir.

Add the 2 tablespoons of water and stir again. Cook gently for about 10 minutes, or until the veggies are softened.

Add the wine and let it bubble, then add the stock, tomatoes, the remaining garlic, the peppercorns and bay leaf.

Add the shanks to the pan and push down so they are covered with liquid. Add a little water if necessary to make sure they're covered.

Cover with a lid and place in the oven. Check after 45 minutes. If the liquid has evaporated too much, top up with a little water. Place the lid back on and cook another hour.

Remove the shanks and keep warm. Mash the tomato mixture with a fork to make a thick sauce. Serve the shanks in bowls topped with the tomato sauce. Serve with the carrot mash.

To make the carrot mash, steam or microwave the carrots until soft. Place in a food processor with the garlic, pepper, salt, butter and yoghurt and process until smooth.

SERVES 4

Lamb korma curry

I unashamedly adore Indian food but takeaway is WAY BOOMBAH. So I was very proud of my beef vindaloo which appeared in my last book. It had half the fat, half the cholesterol and 60 per cent of the calories that a takeaway boombah one had! Woo hoo!

So sticking with traditional fragrant spices, and fresh chilli, ginger and garlic as a base, and by avoiding using ghee and buckets of oil, I give you my lamb korma.

250 g (1 cup) Greek yoghurt
2 teaspoons grated ginger
3 garlic cloves
pinch of sea salt
1 teaspoon ground chilli powder
¼ teaspoon turmeric
1 kg lamb, chopped into cubes
1 tablespoon sunflower oil
1 teaspoon mustard seeds
3 bay leaves
5 cloves
1 teaspoon fenugreek seeds
1 long cinnamon stick
1 large onion, sliced
1 x 400 g tin tomatoes
1 bunch coriander
2–3 sprigs mint, to garnish
1 tablespoon dried or desiccated coconut
1 teaspoon ground coriander
2 teaspoons garam masala
1 tablespoon cumin seeds
1 teaspoon salt
1 teaspoon finely chopped chilli
juice of ½ lemon

Place the yoghurt, ginger, garlic, sea salt, chilli powder and turmeric in a bowl. Add the lamb and marinate for about 1 hour.

Heat the sunflower oil in a non-stick frying pan over medium heat. Add the mustard seeds (careful, they will pop), bay leaves, cloves, fenugreek and cinnamon stick and sauté for about 10–15 seconds. Add the sliced onion and sauté until golden brown.

Process the tomatoes, coriander (including the stems and leaves), mint and coconut in a food processor to a purée.

Add the puréed mixture to the pan along with the ground coriander, garam masala, cumin seeds, salt and chilli.

Add the lamb and 500 ml warm water. Simmer for about 1 hour. Check the meat and cook for longer if necessary, until the meat is very tender.

Just before serving, add the lemon juice and stir through. Serve with cauliflower rice (p 178).

SERVES 4

Beef stroganoff

When I think about daggy dishes mum used to make back in the '70s, this one springs to mind. Not that that it didn't taste great back then, it just conjures up way-boombah creaminess now. But take out the sour cream and use yoghurt instead, forget the buttery, white, tasteless noodles and replace with cauliflower rice and some crunchy green beans and it's a cracking dish!!!

500 g blade steak
sea salt and freshly ground pepper
1 teaspoon sweet paprika
1 large onion, sliced
1 garlic clove, crushed
1½ tablespoons olive oil
12 button mushrooms, quartered
250 ml (1 cup) salt-reduced beef stock
1 tablespoon Worcestershire sauce
4 tablespoons Greek yoghurt
1 tablespoon Dijon mustard
½ teaspoon cayenne pepper
½ teaspoon ground chilli powder
freshly snipped chives, to serve

In a large bowl, season the beef with good pinches of sea salt, pepper and the paprika.

Heat a non-stick frying pan with 1 tablespoon of olive oil and brown the beef in two batches. Remove the beef with a slotted spoon and set aside.

Add another ½ tablespoon of olive oil and add the onion and garlic and sauté over medium-low heat for about 5 minutes.

Add 1 tablespoon of water to add moisture to the pan and stir. Add the mushrooms and cook for another 2 minutes. Add the stock and Worcestershire sauce. Add the beef to the pan and stir through. Cover with a lid and simmer for about 45 minutes.

Take off the lid and cook for a further 10 minutes to let the sauce thicken a little.

Add the yoghurt, mustard, cayenne pepper and ground chilli and stir through. Cook over low heat for another 10 minutes.

Transfer to a warmed serving dish, sprinkle with chopped chives and serve with cauliflower rice (p 178) and just-cooked crunchy green beans.

SERVES 4

Pork chops with red cabbage and fennel

I reckon you can't get more 'comforted' than guilt-free chomping on a pork chop. You're going to have to go with me on this method of cooking. I discovered it via *Cook's Illustrated* when I was researching how to cook pork chops quickly without them drying out. The secret is starting to cook in a cold frying pan.

2 pork chops (fatty rind removed. Yes, please)
sea salt and freshly ground pepper
1-½ tablespoons olive oil
12 sage leaves, shredded
2 tablespoons balsamic vinegar

SALAD
¼ teaspoon fennel seeds
1 teaspoon unsalted butter
½ granny smith apple, grated
½ red cabbage, finely shredded
2 tablespoons red wine vinegar

Dry each chop with paper towel. Season each side with sea salt and pepper. Add the olive oil to a COLD frying pan.

Place the pork chops in the pan and THEN heat to medium heat. Leave for 6 minutes. Do not turn or check during this time. After 6 minutes, turn the chops over, then cover with a lid and cook a further 3 minutes. Remove the chops to rest and add the sage to the pan.

Give the pan a scrape and a stir, then add the balsamic vinegar. After 30 seconds, pour the sage and vinegar over the chops and serve with the red cabbage salad.

To make the salad, heat a non-stick frying pan over medium heat and add the fennel seeds. Cook for 30 seconds, stirring constantly. Add the butter, let it bubble, then add the apple. Let it cook for about 3 minutes.

Add the cabbage and sea salt and pepper and give it another good stir. Cook for 4–5 minutes (I like my cabbage a little crunchy, but cook it longer if you like a 'sauerkraut' consistency). Add the vinegar. Let it cook for about 30 seconds, then serve with the pork chops.

SERVES 2

Eye fillet with Swiss browns and silverbeet

Silverbeet is the daggy cousin of spinach, but I like its firmer texture. It's easy to grow in your garden but make sure, even if you buy it from the market or supermarket, you really give it a good wash and get the grit out!

2 tablespoons olive oil

2 pieces eye fillet steak (about 140 g each)

sea salt and freshly ground pepper

1 teaspoon butter

3 garlic cloves, finely chopped

8 Swiss brown mushrooms, thickly sliced

1 tablespoon light cream

1 tablespoon Greek yoghurt

½ tablespoon chives, chopped

½ tablespoon continental parsley, chopped

1 bunch silverbeet, roughly chopped

1 tablespoon dry white wine

Drizzle 1 teaspoon of olive oil onto each steak and season with sea salt and pepper.

Add the butter, 1 tablespoon of oil and half the chopped garlic in a small non-stick frying pan over low heat and gently melt. When the butter starts bubbling, turn the heat up to medium and add the mushrooms.

Cook the mushrooms, stirring constantly, for about 6–7 minutes. Add the cream, yoghurt, chives, parsley and salt and pepper, and stir through. Let it bubble, then simmer on low for a further 2 minutes. Keep warm.

Heat another frying pan over medium–high heat and when very hot, add the steaks. Cook for 3–4 minutes depending on thickness, then turn and cook the other side.

Remove the steaks from the pan and rest, covered with foil. Keep the juices from the pan.

Heat a large non-stick frying pan over medium heat and add the remaining oil and garlic. Just let the garlic change colour slightly, be careful not to burn.

Add the silverbeet and salt and pepper and with a pair of tongs, keep tossing for about 3–4 minutes then turn off the heat. I like my silverbeet a bit crunchy, but if you like yours softer, cook another 2 minutes or so.

Heat the juices from the rested meat in a frying pan over medium heat. Add the white wine and let it bubble for about 20–30 seconds. If it seems to have evaporated too much, add a tablespoon of water. Keep warm on low.

OK, ready to plate up! Place the silverbeet in a nice 'mound' in the middle of each plate, top with the steak, then with the mushrooms. Drizzle the sauce on top.

SERVES 2

4-hour slow-cooked garlicky lamb

So this is what our mums and grandmothers used to do on a Sunday. They got up at 7 am. Then they'd pop the roast in the oven, get everyone ready for church, come home and have tender, divine lamb you could carve with a fork, ready Freddy by noon. No frigging around. And none of that pink, firm lamb thanks. This is get-out-of-town bloody amazing lamb you simply bung in the oven and take out about 4 hours later. And don't freak out about lamb shoulder. It ain't pretty but it's THE best cut to use for slow-cooked lamb.

1 kg shoulder of lamb
sea salt and freshly ground pepper
olive oil, to drizzle
1 whole bulb garlic
2–3 sprigs rosemary
white wine
375 ml (1½ cups) chicken stock
1 iceberg lettuce, cut into 4 wedges
2 lemons, cut into wedges

Preheat the oven to 230°C. Score the skin of the shoulder about every 2.5 cm. Place the lamb in a large roasting pan. Sprinkle with sea salt and pepper and drizzle with olive oil.

Cut the garlic bulb in half and place under the shoulder to prop it up. Cut the lemons in half and prop those under the lamb. This will act as a 'rack' and help the fat to render off the lamb. Pop the sprigs of rosemary on top of the lamb and cover tightly with foil. As soon as you put the lamb in the oven, turn the heat down to 160°C. Leave to roast slowly for 4 hours.

After 4 hours, remove the foil from the lamb and turn the oven up to 220°C. Roast for a further 20 minutes to crisp up the top of the lamb. Take the lamb out of the oven. Remove from the pan, place on a board and cover with foil. Rest for 15 minutes.

Pour out most of the oil and rosemary from the pan, remove the lemons and squeeze out the soft garlic cloves onto the tray. Add a splash of white wine and the chicken stock and stir well. Let the 'gravy' bubble well, but don't let it evaporate too much. This should take about 5–6 minutes.

Pull the lamb apart and place shredded bits and chunks on a nice big platter and drizzle with the 'gravy'. Add the wedges of iceberg lettuce drizzled with olive oil, a squeeze of lemon juice and sea salt and pepper. Serve with roasted carrots with feta (p 193).

SERVES 6

I'm trying not to sound like a wanker, but organic chicken and duck is the way to go please. And free-range or corn-fed is NOT organic, ok? Not only is the flavour better, the method of production is way more humane. Let your chooks and ducks live like chooks and ducks for at least a while, scratching and pecking around the yard like they should.

My chicken 'parma'

Why do pubs pride themselves on serving chicken parmigiana the size of a small Persian rug? Seriously, the parma could be a pin-up dish for our national obesity problem.

Here's MY parma... a reasonable and satisfying size using almond meal for the crust, a yummy tomato sauce and some bubbling mozzarella cheese.

4 x 140 g skinless chicken breasts
sea salt and freshly ground pepper
150 g almond meal
zest of ½ lemon
3 teaspoons butter
1 tablespoon olive oil
500 g (2 cups) tomato passata
120 g grated light mozzarella cheese
cherry tomatoes, to serve
1 iceberg lettuce, cut into wedges, to serve

Preheat the oven to 180°C. Flatten the chicken breasts and season with sea salt amd pepper.

Pour the almond meal on a plate and add the lemon zest. Coat each chicken breast with the almond meal mixture.

Heat the butter and olive oil in a non-stick frying pan over medium heat. Add the chicken and reduce the heat. Cook the chicken for about 10 minutes on one side, then turn and cook for another 6 minutes. Drain on paper towel.

Transfer the chicken to a glass or porcelain baking dish. Pour over the tomato passata. Sprinkle with cheese and place in the oven.

Bake for about 10 minutes, or until bubbling. It's ready! Serve with cherry tomatoes and some iceberg wedges.

SERVES 4

Chicken cacciatore

I know this screams daggy '70s dinner party but who cares? It's bloody tasty and a perfect non-boombah dish to serve any night of the week.

1½ tablespoons olive oil
4 small skinless chicken thighs
1 skinless chicken breast
sea salt and freshly ground pepper
1 large red capsicum, chopped
1 onion, chopped
3 garlic cloves, finely chopped
185 ml (¾ cup) dry white wine
1 x 240 g tin chopped tomatoes with juice
185 ml (¾ cup) reduced-salt chicken stock
3 tablespoons drained capers
1 teaspoon dried chilli flakes
1 teaspoon dried oregano
8 button mushrooms, quartered
8 kalamata olives, with stones
1 handful flat-leaf parsley, chopped
1 handful basil, chopped

Heat the olive oil in a large heavy-based saucepan over medium–high heat. Season the chicken pieces with sea salt and pepper. Add the chicken to the pan and cook until lightly golden. Transfer the chicken to a plate and set aside.

Add the red capsicum, onion and garlic to the same pan and sauté over medium–low heat for about 5 minutes, or until the onion is tender. Stir constantly as there's not much oil and use a little water if it's sticking.

Add the wine and simmer for about 2 minutes. Add the tomatoes with their juice, stock, capers, chilli and oregano.

Return the chicken pieces to the pan and coat in the sauce. Place the lid on the saucepan and simmer for 1 hour.

About 20 minutes before serving, add the mushrooms and the olives, then cover with the lid.

Remove the chicken pieces and keep warm on a platter. Turn up the heat and cook the sauce, uncovered, for a few minutes until it slightly thickens.

Spoon the sauce over the warm chicken and sprinkle over the parsley and basil. Serve immediately with a crisp iceberg salad.

SERVES 4

Duck and orange

Duck à l'orange has been served around the world for over 100 years. It's a wonderful combination, but like other duck dishes it sings boomberamah to *moi*. So, here's duck breast baked in the oven, with a tangy, orange, zesty sauce, accompanied by the bittersweet combo of a radicchio and red onion salad. *Sans* the calories.

2 duck breasts, on the bone with skin

pinch of five-spice

sea salt and freshly ground pepper

zest of 1 orange, pith removed, sliced into matchsticks

4 tablespoons red wine vinegar

juice of 1 orange

2 shallots, finely chopped

250 ml (1 cup) salt-reduced chicken stock

1 teaspoon butter

RADICCHIO SALAD

1 whole radicchio

1 red onion, finely slices

2 tablespoons olive oil

juice of ½ lemon

sea salt and freshly ground pepper

Preheat the oven to 220°C. Line a roasting tray with baking paper. Season the duck breasts with the five spice and some sea salt and pepper. Place on the tray. Roast for 10 minutes, then reduce the heat to 170°C and roast for another 20 minutes. When cooked, set aside to rest and cover with foil to keep warm.

Meanwhile, to make the raddichio salad, shred the radicchio to a nice coleslaw-like consistency. Toss the onion with the radicchio. Drizzle over the olive oil and lemon juice and season with sea salt and pepper.

Bring some water to the boil in a saucepan and blanch the zesty orange matchsticks for about 5 minutes. Remove and set aside. Tip out the water and add the vinegar, orange juice, shallots, and chicken stock and simmer until the sauce is reduced to a little less than a cup. Add the butter and the orange zest and stir through.

To serve, slice the duck into three or four slices on the diagonal.

Drizzle over the orange sauce and serve with braised lettuce (p 186) and the radicchio salad.

SERVES 4

Piri piri chicken

I was almost going to say that of all the takeaway options, Portuguese-style chicken is pretty good. But when you can make the sauce at home (and it keeps in the fridge if you make lots) and you know EXACTLY what's gone into the piri piri sauce, well, why would you bother?? (Don't answer.)

There are a million recipes for piri piri sauce and this is a combination of about four or five I've tested. If you want HOT, then add more chillies. If you are a wuss, use less. And one more thing… even though you can cook this dish in the oven, it tastes ten times better on the barbecue.

PIRI PIRI SAUCE
10 red chillies
1 garlic clove, finely chopped
1 teaspoon sea salt
½ teaspoon dried oregano
½ tablespoon paprika
juice of 1 lime
100 ml olive oil
30 ml red wine vinegar
1 whole organic chicken, which you will have spatchcocked (this is easy, see p118)
sea salt and freshly ground pepper

Preheat the oven to 190°C. Put the chillies on a baking tray and roast for 10 minutes. Remove from the oven, leave to cool, then roughly chop.

Place the chillies, garlic, salt, oregano, paprika, lime juice, olive oil and vinegar in a saucepan and simmer for 2–3 minutes. Allow the mixture to cool, then blend it to a purée using a food processor.

Season the spatchcocked chicken with sea salt and pepper and place in a sealable plastic bag. Add half the piri piri sauce, squishing it evenly around the chicken. Marinate in the refrigerator for at least 1 hour (but 2 would be excellent).

Heat a large non-stick frying pan over medium–high heat. Cook the chicken for about 3 minutes on each side, or until golden.

Transfer the chicken to a roasting dish and roast in the oven for 30 minutes, or until cooked through.

Alternatively, place the chicken on a barbecue hotplate heated to medium. Cover with the barbecue lid and cook for 10–15 minutes on both sides or until cooked through, basting regularly with the remaining piri-piri sauce.

SERVES 4

How to spatchcock (or butterfly) a chicken

Rinse your chicken well and pat dry inside and out with paper towel.

Trim off excess any excess fat around the cavity opening.

Using kitchen shears or a very sharp boning knife, cut along each side of the backbone and remove.

Spread open the bird a little and you'll see and feel the keel bone at the top inside cavity and the cartlidge that runs between the breasts. You want to remove these. Using the knife, make an incision around each side of the keel bone and cut along both sides of the cartlidge. Push down on the bird, grab the keel bone and remove the keel bone and the cartlidge together.

Cut off any more excess fat to neaten up.

Now to make it easier to work with, cut right through the bird to give you two halves. You'll have to cut through the wishbone which you can just remove.

There may be a little excess cartlidge along each side of the bird — just trim this off. Your bird is now ready for basting!

The best roast chicken with thanks to Thomas Keller

US chef Thomas Keller runs some of that country's most celebrated restaurants. And yet I reckon this simple dish is one of his best. Good old roast chicken. Trust me, the guy knows how to roast a chook and, with this recipe, you can't go wrong. I've adjusted it slightly... he uses Kosher salt but I prefer sea salt and Thomas uses butter. I don't think it needs it! Follow the instructions to the letter. Yes, the oven is THAT hot. And YES, you serve the chicken with Dijon mustard!

1 whole organic chicken (about 1.5 kg), washed and dried thoroughly

sea salt and freshly ground pepper

2–3 thyme sprigs

Dijon mustard, to serve

Preheat the oven to 230°C. Dry the chicken inside and out with paper towel. Truss the chicken by tying up the legs and wings nice and close to the bird.

Now here's the bit I love. Thomas says to "rain" salt over the bird. So do it (it's about 1 tablespoon). Add some pepper. That's it. Pop it in the oven and leave for 50 minutes.

Remove from the oven and rest. Sprinkle over with thyme leaves. Baste the juices over the chicken, including the thyme leaves. Leave for 15 minutes.

To serve, cut the breast down the middle and serve it on the bone, with one wing joint still attached to each. It's not supposed to be fancy looking. Serve with mustard on the side and a simple iceberg salad.

SERVES 4

My Peking duck

Mmmmmm, PEKING DUCK. Sadly, whopping pieces of fatty duck with crispy duck skin, sugary plum sauce and white processed pancakes don't like my belly (and I'm guessing yours).

But what if you used duck with a hint of spicy skin, a thin, light omelette instead of the pancake, and a sauce that has the punch of plum but not the sugary glugginess? Wouldn't you want to thank me??

2 duck breasts, with the bone and skin on
pinch of sea salt
pinch of white pepper
pinch of ground cumin
pinch of ground coriander
pinch of ground cinnamon
pinch of ground chilli
1 continental cucumber, cut into 10 cm sticks
1 bunch spring onions, cut into 10 cm sticks

SAUCE
2 tablespoons sesame oil
4 tablespoons apple balsamic vinegar (found in specialty food stores)
1 tablespoon lemon juice
1 tablespoon light soy sauce or tamari
pinch of white pepper
pinch of dried chilli flakes

PANCAKES
4 eggs
sunflower oil, for cooking

Preheat the oven to 220°C. Place the duck breasts on a baking tray. Sprinkle the salt, pepper, cumin, coriander, cinnamon and chilli over the duck. You don't need to add any oil.

Roast in the oven at 220°C for 10 minutes, then turn the heat down to 170°C and roast for 30 minutes more. Take the duck out of the oven and leave to rest before slicing into 12 slices (6 a breast). Set aside.

To make the sauce, combine the sesame oil, vinegar, lemon juice, soy sauce, pepper and chilli flakes. Set aside.

To make the pancakes, whisk the eggs together with 3 tablespoons of water. Heat a non-stick frying pan over medium heat. Add about 1 tablespoon of sunflower oil and a spoonful of the mixture, or enough to make a nice small pancake. Flip after 1 minute and cook for a another 30 seconds. Remove from the pan and place on a plate.

Cover the pancake with paper towel. Repeat with the remaining mixture to make 12 pancakes in total. After 6 'pancakes', add another tablespoon of sunflower oil to the pan.

To serve, place the duck, 1 piece of cucumber, 1 spring onion and a drizzle of the sauce on a pancake and roll up. Use the sauce to dip in.

SERVES 6

I'm so curious as to why some of my friends are terrified about cooking fish. When did we get so scaredy-cat about heating a pan, adding a little oil or butter, placing in a piece of seasoned fish or prawns, turning after a few minutes, leaving for another minute or two, then serving? Mussels simply open themselves like magic after you cover them with a lid. And when was the last time you really had to shuck an oyster yourself? I blame the TV chefs who always give us the willies with the warning, 'Don't overcook the fish'. Ok! We won't!!

Oysters four ways

HOT SYDNEY ROCKS

12 freshly shucked Sydney rock oysters
2 chillies, finely chopped
2 garlic cloves, finely chopped
1 knob of ginger, peeled and finely chopped
2 kaffir lime leaves, finely shredded
sesame oil
light soy sauce or tamari
squeeze of lime juice

Fill a pot halfway with water and bring to the boil. Turn down the heat and simmer. Set the oysters on a steamer plate or in a bamboo steamer that will fit over the saucepan.

Sprinkle the chilli, garlic, ginger and kaffir lime leaves evenly between the oysters. Add a few drops of sesame oil to each oyster, then add a splash of soy. Finish with a few drops of lime juice on each.

Cover and place plate or steamer over boiling water and steam for 6–8 minutes.

Alternatively, to cook in the oven, preheat the oven to 200°C. Line a baking tray with baking paper and place the oysters on the tray. Cook for about 10 minutes, or until the oysters just start to 'bubble'.

OYSTERS WITH WASABI MAYONNAISE (per dozen)

1 tablespoon light mayonnaise
1 tablespoon Greek yoghurt
wasabi paste, to taste

Combine the ingredients and place a dollop on each oyster. Serve with lime wedges.

OYSTERS WITH CHARDONNAY AND SPICY WATERMELON (per dozen)

2 cups chopped watermelon
125 ml (½ cup) Chardonnay
1 teaspoon sea salt
1 teaspoon sugar
1 red chilli, finely chopped
2 tablespoons lime juice
¼ teaspoon lime zest

Mash the watermelon with a fork, just to break it down. Don't turn it into juice.

Pour the mixture into a bowl and add the Chardonnay, salt, sugar, chilli, lime juice and lime zest.

Pour the mixture into a metal baking tin and freeze for a few hours, occasionally breaking it up with a fork.

When ready to serve, using a fork, scrape the frozen mixture into a teaspoon-size ball and place it on top of each oyster. Serve immediately.

OYSTERS WITH HORSERADISH AND PARMESAN (per dozen)

2 tablespoons horseradish cream

70 g grated parmesan cheese

1 tablespoon Greek yoghurt

1 tablespoon finely chopped flat-leaf parsley

sea salt and freshly ground pepper

Preheat the oven to 200°C. In a small bowl, combine the parmesan, horseradish, yoghurt parsley and salt and pepper.

Place the oysters on a baking tray lined with baking paper. Top each oyster with a teaspoon of the mixture.

Bake until the cheese is golden and bubbling. Serve immediately.

Crispy-skinned salmon with roasted asparagus and baby tomatoes

8 large cherry tomatoes

8 asparagus spears, woody ends trimmed

2 garlic cloves, chopped

1 tablespoon olive oil, plus extra for drizzling

sea salt and freshly ground pepper

4 salmon fillets (about 150 g each), skin on

squeeze of lemon juice

Preheat the oven to 180°C. Line a baking tray with baking paper.

Place the tomatoes, asparagus, garlic, olive oil and salt and pepper in a bowl and mix until the veggies are well coated. Place the veggies on the tray and roast for about 10 minutes. Keep warm.

Meanwhile, prepare the salmon by rubbing some olive oil into the skin of the fish and season with sea salt and pepper.

Heat a non-stick frying pan over medium–high heat,. When the pan is hot, place the salmon SKIN SIDE down into the pan.

Leave to cook for 3 minutes (don't try and turn it before then). NOW turn. Cook a further 2 minutes, then remove from the pan and transfer the salmon to two plates.

Serve the salmon immediately with the tomatoes and asparagus.

SERVES 4

Mussels with tomato, white wine and garlic

1 tablespoon olive oil

1 large onion, finely chopped

3 garlic cloves, chopped

150 ml dry white wine

1 x 400 g tin chopped tomatoes

1 bay leaf

1 teaspoon dried chilli flakes

sea salt and freshly ground pepper

24 mussels, washed and debearded

2 tablespoons chopped flat-leaf parsley

Heat the olive oil in a large saucepan over medium heat. Add the onions and garlic and fry gently for about 5 minutes.

Add the white wine and let it sizzle, then add the tomatoes, bay leaf, chilli and sea salt and pepper. Let it bubble, then turn down the heat and gently simmer for about 10 minutes.

Turn the heat back up, add the mussels and cover with a lid. Leave to boil for about 5 minutes, or until the shells open. Discard any unopened shells.

Serve in big warmed bowls and sprinkle with parsley to garnish.

SERVES 4

Prawn and asparagus red curry

Here's a fast, flashy, hot curry using prawns and crunchy asparagus. Don't know what it is, but they go together so well. Using only a tiny bit of light coconut milk and a little oil, this makes a low-calorie, tasty, non-boombah dinner. I think we have this at least once a week in summer!

6 asparagus spears
6 spring onions
1 tablespoon sunflower oil
1 teaspoon sesame oil
1 garlic clove, finely chopped
1 red chilli, finely chopped
1 knob of ginger, peeled and finely chopped
1 large onion, chopped into large pieces
2 heaped tablespoons red curry paste
20 prawns, cleaned, shelled, deveined, tail intact
3 tablespoons light coconut milk
1 tablespoon fish sauce
juice of 1 lime
2 kaffir lime leaves, very finely shredded
lime wedges and coriander leaves, to serve

Trim the woody ends off the asparagus and chop each stalk in half. Trim the dark green ends and the tops off the spring onions and slice each one lengthwise so you have a 'skinnier' spring onion. Cut in half again, so they match in size with the asparagus.

Heat the oils in a non-stick frying pan over medium heat. Add the garlic, chilli and ginger and cook for about 1 minute, stirring constantly so it doesn't burn. Add the onion and stir for a further 1 minute. Add the red curry paste (careful, it will spit) and stir constantly for a further 1 minute.

Add the prawns and stir-fry for about 2 minutes, or until they change colour. Add the coconut milk, 185 ml (¾ cup) water, fish sauce, lime juice and kaffir lime leaves. Stir well, then turn the heat down to a simmer. Cover with a lid and cook for about 3 minutes.

Take the lid off, add the asparagus, stir and cover with the lid. Cook a further 3 minutes, then take the lid off.

Add the spring onion, stir through and let the pan gently bubble for a further 1 minute.

Serve on a warmed platter, with lime wedges and coriander.

SERVES 4

Paella

2 small skinless chicken breast fillets (about 140 g each)

1 chicken Maryland

sea salt and freshly ground pepper

2 tablespoons olive oil

6 slices pancetta, rind removed and chopped

1 onion, finely diced

4 garlic cloves, finely chopped

2 small red chillies, finely chopped

250 ml (1 cup) dry white wine

500 g (2 cups) tomato passata

1 teaspoon smoked paprika

1 red capsicum, chopped

3 pinches of saffron, infused in a little hot water

500 ml (2 cups) salt-reduced chicken stock

1 cauliflower, cut into florets

12 mussels, washed and debearded

10 large prawns, cleaned, shelled, deveined

10–12 calamari rings

3 spring onions, finely sliced

1 large handful flat-leaf parsley, finely chopped

lemon wedges, to serve

Preheat the oven to 190°C. Line a baking tray with baking paper.

Cut each chicken breast into 4 pieces. Separate the leg from the Maryland and the thigh. Season the chicken with sea salt and pepper.

Heat 1 tablespoon of the olive oil in a large non-stick frying pan over medium heat. Add the chicken and cook for 5 minutes, or until browned. Transfer the chicken to the baking tray and roast for about 35 minutes.

Discard the pan juices from the frying pan. Return the frying pan back to the heat and add the remaining olive oil and pancetta and cook until brown and crispy. Remove and set aside. Turn the heat down a little and add the onion, garlic, and chilli. Cook for about 5 minutes, or until the onion softens.

Pour in the wine and stir for 1 minute. Add the passata, paprika, capsicum and the infused saffron and then add half the stock, a little at a time. Let it bubble.

Cook the caulifower in the microwave for 5 minutes, then add to the pan and stir through.

Add the mussels, prawns and calamari, then add the rest of the stock. Cover the pan with a lid or foil and cook for about 5–7 minutes, or until the mussels open. (Discard any unopened shells.)

With the lid off, add the roasted cooked chicken and the pancetta to the pan, then sprinkle over the spring onion and the parsley.

Serve straight from the frying pan with wedges of lemon.

SERVES 4–6

Mussels with coconut and Thai basil

1 tablespoon sunflower oil

1 garlic clove, chopped

1 small red chilli, finely chopped

1 tablespoon Thai green curry paste

3 tablespoons light coconut milk

300 ml salt-reduced chicken stock

squeeze of lime juice

1 teaspoon fish sauce

1 teaspoon brown sugar

24 mussels, washed and debearded

2 tablespoons chopped Thai basil, to garnish

Heat the sunflower oil in a heavy-based saucepan over medium heat. Add the garlic and chilli and stir for about 30 seconds, taking care not to burn. Add the curry paste, stirring constantly (careful, it'll spit!).

Add the coconut milk, then the stock and stir well. Add the lime juice, fish sauce and sugar. Stir well, then add the mussels.

Cover with a lid and cook for about 5 minutes, or until the shells open. Discard any unopened shells.

Remove the mussels with a slotted spoon and divide between two big warmed bowls. Spoon a ladleful of the coconut Thai broth over each bowl and sprinkle with the fresh Thai basil. Serve immediately.

SERVES 2

Tuna mornay

Big memory blast this one. Lunch of tuna mornay with my grandmother, Auntie Val and Mum. Depending on whose house it was, you would get a different version: one had no egg or asparagus, one had the egg only and one had asparagus only. I say add the lot!

1 x 300 g tin tuna in springwater, drained
1 red onion, finely chopped
1 tablespoon chopped flat-leaf parsley
squeeze of lemon juice
2 tablespoons Greek yoghurt
sea salt and freshly ground pepper
2 hard-boiled eggs
8 cooked asparagus spears
35 g (⅓ cup) almond meal
50 g (½ cup) grated parmesan cheese
60 g (½ cup) grated tasty cheese
2 teaspoons butter

Preheat the oven to 190°C. Combine the tuna, onion, parsley, lemon juice, yoghurt and some sea salt and pepper in a bowl.

Slice the egg and arrange on the bottom of a casserole dish. Spread the tuna mixture on top of the egg.

Arrange the asparagus spears in a row. Sprinkle over the almond meal, then top with the cheese. Break up the teaspoons of butter into smaller portions and dot over the top.

Bake for 20–25 minutes, or until bubbling. Serve immediately.

SERVES 4

Fish and zucchini chips with tartare sauce

100 g (1 cup) almond meal

sea salt and freshly ground pepper

8 flathead or whiting fillets

olive oil

lemon or lime wedges, to serve

TARTARE SAUCE

1 tablespoon Greek yoghurt

1 tablspoon light mayonnaise

1 tablespoon chopped cornichons (little dill pickles)

½ tablespoon capers, rinsed and chopped

1 tablespoon chopped flat-leaf parsley

Place the almond meal on a large plate and season with a pinch of sea salt and pepper.

Coat each fish fillet lightly with the almond meal and set aside.

Heat the olive oil and butter in a non-stick frying pan over medium heat. Add the fish and cook for about 3 minutes, then carefully turn and cook for another 3 minutes. Remove from the pan and place on paper towel.

To make the tartare sauce, combine all the ingredients in a small bowl and refrigerate until ready to serve.

Serve the fish with tartare sauce and zucchini 'chips' (p 24).

SERVES 4

COMFORT

CLASSICS

You're feeling down, you're feeling up, you want to commiserate, you want to celebrate. What do we do at these times in our lives? We tend to turn to comfort food. But comfort food has been hijacked – it's morphed into a high-calorie, super-sized indulgence that makes us feel guilty and fat.

I want to give you back the feeling of comfort without the calories, so here's my version of the comfort classics: cheesy pizza, bubbling lasagne and moussaka, tasty burgers and ta da – fried 'rice'. I'll be honest, there's no pasta, rice, batter or pastry here. But trust me, these meals taste really, really good.

Pizza

Yes, PIZZA. Listen up. Takeaway pizza is boombah. I don't care which gluten-free, thin-crust, soy-beaned pizza you've discovered. It won't do your tight jeans any justice.

Please try this and see what you reckon. The base is made from grated ZUCCHINI. After cooking, you let it cool then proceed with the pizza base as you would a regular boombah one. Feel free to try different toppings. One of my other favorite toppings is Napolitana — black olives, mozzarella and anchovies. YUM!!

1 large zucchini, peeled

1 egg

100 g grated light mozzarella cheese, plus extra

2–3 tablespoons tomato passata

2–3 thin slices prosciutto

1 small handful rocket

Preheat the oven to 190°C. Line a shallow baking tray or pizza tray with baking paper.

Peel the zucchini, then grate into a mixing bowl. Whisk the egg and add to the zucchini. Add the grated cheese and mix well.

Pour the mixture onto the tray and bake for about 15 minutes, or until a pale gold colour.

Remove from the oven and, leaving on the baking paper, lift off the tray and leave to cool.

Turn the oven up to 220°C.

Spread the passata over the zucchini base (as you would to a pizza base), then top with cheese, then prosciutto. Bake until the cheese is bubbling. Sprinkle over some rocket. Cut into wedges and serve.

MAKES 1 PIZZA/SERVES 2

Lamb souvlaki

Late-night memories. Out clubbing (ok, it's a VERY distant memory). 2 am. Starving. Pit stop for a souvlaki. Devour in minutes. Then feel like CRAP. I seriously have associated souvlaki with late-night, takeaway boombah food. But grilled lamb with tasty herbs, tomato and tzatziki in a light wrap? Almost makes me want to eat this version sitting on the boot of my car!

2 lamb fillets, cut into cubes
juice of ½ lemon
2 garlic cloves, crushed
1 tablespoon olive oil
1 teaspoon rosemary, finely chopped
1 teaspoon dried oregano
sea salt and freshly ground pepper
1 large zucchini
1 egg
110 g (¾ cup) light grated mozzarella cheese
1 red onion, finely sliced
1 large tomato, chopped
lemon wedges, to serve

TZATZIKI
250 g (1 cup) Greek yoghurt
2 garlic cloves, finely chopped
squeeze of lemon juice
1 continental cucumber, peeled, grated
pinch of sea salt

Preheat the oven to 190°C. Line a shallow baking tray with baking paper. Soak 4 bamboo skewers in cold water.

Place the lamb, lemon juice, garlic, oil, rosemary, oregano and some sea salt and pepper in a ziplock bag. Squish around, then place in the fridge and leave to marinate for about 30 minutes.

Peel the zucchini, then grate into a mixing bowl. Whisk the egg and add to the zucchini. Add the cheese and mix well.

Pour the mixture onto the prepared tray and bake for about 15 minutes, or until a pale gold colour.

Remove from the oven, and leaving on the baking paper, lift off the baking tray and leave to cool. Cut into rectangles, as your 'pita' bread.

Heat a non-stick frying pan over medium heat. Thread the lamb onto the bamboo skewers. Cook the lamb for about 4 minutes on one side and 3 minutes on the other. Remove from the pan and leave to rest.

To make the tzatziki, combine all the ingredients in a small bowl and refrigerate until needed.

To serve, take your 'pita', add a skewer of lamb, some chopped tomato, red onion and a dollop of tzatziki. Serve with lemon wedges.

SERVES 4

Boombah-free burgers

Using my beloved iceberg lettuce cups, these are a favourite Sunday night treat at our joint. Now don't have a fit, but I prefer to use mince with a little bit of fat, not your lean, lean mince. This is, of course, for flavour and apart from a pinch of sea salt, that's it. I find you don't have to add sugary sauces and breadcrumbs and onions etc. to jazz it up. This turns out a true beef burger… juicy and tasty.

500 g beef mince

sea salt and freshly ground pepper

1 tablepoon olive oil

1 large red onion, halved and thinly sliced

1 large ripe tomato, sliced

1 iceberg lettuce

1 slice of tasty cheese per person

1 tablespoon Dijon mustard

½ tablespoon light mayonnaise

½ tablespoon Greek yoghurt

Take a small handful of beef and mold it into a patty. Sprinkle each burger with a little sea salt.

Heat the olive oil in a non-stick frying pan or grill over medium–high heat and cook the burgers until cooked through.

Prepare the iceberg lettuce 'cups' as you would san choy bau (gently take off the large leaves, trim and refrigerate until ready).

Assemble your burger in any order you like! Serve with a dollop of mustardy mayo by combining the mustard, mayonnaise and yoghurt.

SERVES 4

Moussaka

So here's a ripping non-boombah version of moussaka. You know, that delicious, fragrant, cheesy, white-saucy almost national dish of Greece? Well, this version has less fat and lower calories than the traditional one!!

3 long thin eggplants, cut lengthways
sea salt and freshly ground pepper
3 tablespoons olive oil
500 g lamb mince
1 large onion, chopped
1 garlic clove, chopped
1 carrot, chopped
125 ml (½ cup) white wine
1 teaspoon dried oregano
½ teaspoon allspice
½ teaspoon ground cinnamon
pinch of nutmeg
½ teaspoon ground cumin
pinch of cayenne pepper
250 g (1 cup) tomato passata
1 bay leaf

'BECHAMEL SAUCE'
300 g light Greek yoghurt
2 eggs
pinch of nutmeg
sea salt and white pepper
35 g (⅓ cup) grated parmesan cheese
30 g feta cheese

Preheat the oven to 180°C. Place the eggplant on a tray lined with baking paper. Sprinkle with sea salt and drizzle with olive oil.

Bake for about 20 minutes. Take out of the oven and, keeping the eggplant on the baking paper, slide off the tray and set aside.

Heat 1 tablespoon of the olive oil in a non-stick frying pan over medium heat. Add the mince and lightly brown. Remove from the pan with a slotted spoon and set aside.

Pour off the liquid and using the same pan, add the 1 tablespoon of the olive oil. Add the onion and cook for about 5 minutes, or until transluscent.

Add the garlic, carrot and 1 tablespoon of water and cook for another 5 minutes.

Add the wine and let it sizzle, then add the lamb mince, oregano, allspice, cinnamon, nutmeg, cumin, cayenne pepper and sea salt and pepper. Stir through. Add the tomato passata and bay leaf.

Turn the heat down to a simmer, pop the lid on and cook for about 30 minutes, stirring occasionally. Take off the lid and cook a further 10 minutes to let some of the liquid evaporate.

Line a large ovenproof baking dish with some slices of eggplant. Top with a layer of the meat mixture. Add another layer of eggplant and the rest of the meat mixture.

To make the white sauce, combine the yoghurt and eggs. Add the nutmeg, and a pinch of sea salt and white pepper. Pour the mixture over the meat and sprinkle with the parmesan and feta.

Bake for about 35 minutes, or until golden brown and the cheese sauce is bubbling.

SERVES 4–6

Texas chilli con carne

Everyone seems to have a favourite recipe for chilli con carne. For too long my recipe relied on the assistance of a certain 'yee ha' brand of taco or chilli seasoning mix found in supermarkets. I wanted my own recipe, with no surprises, so I got to setting up my science lab and broke down the ingredients in the packet.

Red kidney beans are all a bit too carby overload for me, so I make my chilli without beans. But it's not that unusual… they've been onto this for years in the heart of chilli land — Texas. They even have a name for it. Yep, Texas chilli.

1 tablespoon olive oil

450 g minced beef

1 large onion, chopped

2 garlic cloves, finely chopped

1 tablespoon dried onion

1 teaspoon garlic powder

1 teaspoon ground cumin

1 teaspoon paprika

1 teaspoon onion powder

1 teaspoon sea salt

½ teaspoon sugar

1 teaspoon cocoa powder

1 teaspoon dried oregano

½ teaspoon cayenne pepper

½ teaspoon dried chilli flakes

250 g (1 cup) tomato passata

1 x 400 g tin tomatoes, crushed

300 ml salt-reduced beef stock

1 bay leaf

freshly ground pepper

200 ml light Greek yoghurt

Heat the oil in a large saucepan over medium heat. Gently cook the onion and garlic. Add all the dried spices to the mixture and stir for 1 minute, or until you can smell the lovely aromas.

Add the beef and cook until it just changes colour. Add the tomato passata and tinned tomatoes and cook for about 5 minutes, stirring often.

Pour in the beef stock, add the bay leaf and some pepper and bring to the boil. Turn down the heat and simmer for about 20–25 minutes, stirring occasionally.

To serve, ladle the chilli into warmed bowls, add a dollop of yoghurt and a parmesan crisp (p 55).

SERVES 4

Lasagne

It's gotta be THE most boombah Italian food you could chow down on. Layer upon layer of thick, white pasta sheets, groaning with meat and gallons of cheesy sauce. I love it, but it doesn't love my butt. Not to be daunted, I was determined to get that lasagne kick without the chumba wumba.

So here it is. Delicious meat sauce between layers of roasted zucchini, topped with mozzarella and parmesan. Trust me, anything that comes out of the oven bubbling and spluttering gives you a ripping 'comfort' hit.

3 zucchini
sea salt and freshly ground pepper
1–2 tablespoons olive oil
1 tablespoon olive oil
100 g pancetta
1 onion, finely chopped
1 carrot, finely chopped
2 garlic cloves, finely chopped
2 sprigs rosemary, finely chopped
2 bay leaves
2 sprigs thyme, finely chopped
400 g coarsely minced beef
200 g coarsely minced pork
2 x 400 g tins tomatoes
185 ml (¾ cup) red wine
200 g grated mozzarella cheese
100 g grated parmesan cheese

Preheat the oven to 180°C. Slice the zucchini lengthways and place on baking paper on a baking tray. Sprinkle with sea salt, pepper and a drizzle of olive oil and bake for about 20 minutes. Don't let it soften too much. Remove from the oven and leave to cool.

Heat the oil in a large non-stick frying pan and cook the pancetta until it just turns colour.

Add the onion, carrot, garlic, rosemary, bay leaves and thyme and cook until the veggies soften a little.

Add the beef and pork and cook for about 5 minutes, or until the meat changes colour.

Add the wine and let it sizzle, then add the tomato and 500 ml (2 cups) water and bring to the boil. Turn the heat right down and simmer with the lid on for about an hour and a half.

To assemble the lasagna, take the zucchini slices and place a layer on the base of an ovenproof dish. Add a layer of the meat sauce and sprinkle a layer of mozzarella cheese on top of the meat. Add another layer of zucchini, a final layer of meat and sprinkle the remaining mozzarella and the parmesan on top. Bake for about 35–40 minutes, or until golden and bubbly.

SERVES 6

Authentic Bolognese ragu

I know you'll all have your own special Bolognese recipe… you might use beef mince, tomato paste, carrots and garlic, some of you may add a little sugar, some red wine or even cinnamon! I also had my own recipe… that is until I actually WENT TO BOLOGNA. Yep, THE home of Bolognese sauce. And get this. They are so obsessed with protecting the integrity of the recipe that in 1982 the Bolognese chapter of the Accademia Italiana della Cucina decreed THIS is the official recipe.

For a start, it's much paler than the bright red-staining gunk we're used to. And they use veal and pork mince — it's softer and has a lovely flavour. Oh, and they add MILK. But before you scoff, as an experiment, why don't you give it a try? If you use wonderful spaghetti squash when it's in season, man it's good! If you can't get spaghetti squash, try peeled ribbons of steamed zucchini or carrot. And top with a little shaved parmesan.

400 g ground lean veal
300 g ground lean pork
sea salt and freshly ground pepper
1 tablespoon olive oil
150 g pancetta, finely diced
1 onion, diced
1 carrot, diced
2 celery sticks, diced
2 bay leaves
300 ml dry white wine
400 g tomato passata
4 tablespoons salt-reduced beef stock
300 ml skim milk

Combine the two meats with a little sea salt and pepper and set aside, covered, in the fridge.

Heat the olive oil in a large heavy-based saucepan over low heat. Cook the pancetta over a low flame until the fat starts to melt. Add the onion and cook for about 5 minutes. Don't let the onion turn golden.

Add the carrot, celery and bay leaves and cook for a further 5 minutes, stirring continuously.

Turn the heat up and add the white wine. Let it sizzle. Add the meat and cook until the meat just starts to change colour.

Add the passata and stock to the pot. Turn down the flame and simmer uncovered for about 2 hours. If it looks like it's losing too much moisture, add a bit more stock.

After about 2 hours, add the milk, a little at a time, stirring and cooking over a low heat for a further 45 minutes.

Season to taste and serve with steamed spaghetti squash, or steamed ribbons of zucchini or carrot.

SERVES 6

Fried 'rice'

We used to take a couple of empty saucepans to the local Chinese restaurant when I was a kid, and they'd fill it with sticky, sickly, battered sweet and sour pork and masses of calorie-laden, carb-loaded fried rice. I certainly don't miss the pork concoction, but I love a good fried rice.

So relying on my trusty companion the cauliflower, I've used a cauliflower rice recipe combined with the yum elements of fried rice — some egg, spring onion and a bit of ham off the bone. Add a sprinkle of soy sauce, and you get the vibe of the traditional dish, without the calories.

1 cauliflower, cut into florets

1–½ tablespoons peanut oil

2 eggs, lightly whisked

2 garlic cloves, finely chopped

1 small knob of fresh ginger, cut into small strips

1 small red chilli, finely chopped

1 onion, finely chopped

100 g leg ham or lean bacon, cut into long thin strips

100 g green prawns, cleaned, shelled, deveined and chopped (optional)

2 tablespoons light soy sauce or tamari

2 spring onions, trimmed and sliced on the diagonal

90 g bean sprouts

extra spring onion, for serving, finely shredded

Place the cauliflower in a microwave dish and cook on high for about 4 minutes. Do not add any water. Place in a food processor and process until it resembles couscous or rice. Transfer to a baking tray and place in the refrigerator to cool.

Heat ½ tablespoon of the peanut oil in a wok or frying pan over medium heat. Add the eggs and cook for about 1 minute, or until they are lightly scrambled. Remove from the wok and set aside on paper towel.

Add the rest of the oil and cook the garlic, ginger and chilli for about 20 seconds. Add the onion and stir, cooking for about 30 seconds.

Add the ham or bacon and cook until it starts turning golden. Add the prawns and cauliflower and toss through the pan.

Chop the egg into small pieces and add to the wok. Add the soy sauce, then the spring onions and bean shoots and stir through. Sprinkle with the extra spring onions and serve.

SERVES 4

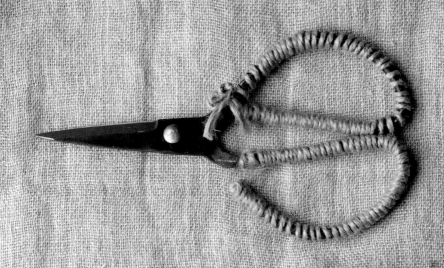

I'm still seriously freaked out when I hear an adult proclaim they don't eat or like vegetables. It's lazy and boring and clichéd.

Sesame seeds, fresh herbs, cumin, chilli flakes or parmesan cheese can transform an ordinary piece of pumpkin or a carrot or a zucchini into something special. Simply adding garlic, cracked pepper, sea salt and olive oil to spinach or silverbeet or broccoli can be a dish in itself.

Start looking at cooking vegetables as a meal. Relax, it doesn't mean you've turned vegetarian.

Brussels sprouts with pine nuts and bacon

400 g Brussels sprouts, tops cut off, halved

1 tablespoon olive oil

1 red onion, chopped

2 garlic cloves

80 g (½ cup) pine nuts

2 sprigs thyme, chopped

120 g bacon, chopped

1 tablespoon lemon juice

2 tablespoons dry white wine

sea salt and freshly ground pepper

Bring a small saucepan filled with salted water to the boil over medium heat. Add the sprouts and cook for about 5 minutes. Drain immediately so they don't continue to cook.

Heat the olive oil in a non-stick frying pan and cook the onion, garlic, pine nuts, thyme and bacon, stirring continously.

When the bacon has changed colour, add the lemon juice and white wine. Let it sizzle and add the sprouts. Cook until they are heated through. Transfer to a warmed dish and serve.

SERVES 4

Cauliflower rice

½ **cauliflower**

Cut the cauliflower into small florets and place in a microwave-safe container with a lid. Do not add water. Microwave on 100% power for 5 minutes.

Using a hand-held blender, whizz the cauliflower until it starts to resemble rice. Alternatively, pulse it in bursts in a food processor. Serve immediately.

SERVES 2

Spicy roasted pumpkin

1 jap pumpkin, cut into 'crescents'
1 teaspoon chilli flakes
1 teaspoon cumin seeds
1 teaspoon sea salt
1 teaspoon peppercorns
1 ½ tablespoons olive oil

To make the roasted pumpkin, preheat the oven to 180°C. Line a baking tray with baking paper. Place the 'crescents' on the tray, standing upright. Place all the spices in a mortar and pestle and pound them until they are crushed. Pour the olive oil over the pumpkin and then sprinkle over the spice mix.

Roast for 35–40 minutes, or until the pumpkin is slightly brown and just soft.

SERVES 4

Parsnip purée

6–8 parsnips, peeled, stringy cores removed,
and chopped

1 tablespoon olive oil

sea salt and freshly ground pepper

⅛ teaspoon nutmeg

Preheat the oven to 200°C. Peel the parsnips, and lay them on baking paper on a baking tray. Drizzle with olive oil and sprinkle with sea salt and pepper.

Roast in the oven for 20–25 minutes, or until they turn lightly golden, turning them once halfway through cooking.

Remove from the oven and place the parsnips into a food processor. Add 250 ml (1 cup) water a little at a time and pulse until puréed to the desired consistency. Add the nutmeg and salt and pepper.

SERVES 4–6

Baked fennel

I'm going to use the word 'caramelise' here, which sounds delicious and that's just what happens when the fennel roasts in the olive oil. Baked fennel this way goes so well with everything from chicken to fish.

3 fennel bulbs

1 tablespoon olive oil

5 garlic cloves, unpeeled

sea salt and freshly ground pepper

40 g grated parmesan cheese

Cut the stems off the fennel, then slice in half lengthways. Cut into quarters and place on a baking tray lined with baking paper, cut side down.

Drizzle with olive oil, toss over the unpeeled garlic cloves and sea salt and pepper.

Roast for about 30 minutes, then turn and cook for a further 30 minutes. Sprinkle with some parmesan cheese, roast for a further 5 minutes. Serve immediately.

SERVES 4

Braised lettuce

1 large cos lettuce, cut into 6 pieces, or 6 baby
cos lettuce

150 g pancetta or good-quality bacon, diced

1 tablespoon olive oil

2 onions, chopped

5 garlic cloves, crushed

2 carrots, chopped

2 sprigs thyme, chopped

sea salt and freshly ground pepper

40 ml dry white wine

500 ml salt-reduced chicken stock

Preheat the oven to 160°C. Blanch the lettuce in a pot of boiling water for about 30 seconds. Shake off the excess water and set aside.

In a non-stick frying pan, gently brown the pancetta in the olive oil. Add the onion, garlic and carrots and cook until the vegetables just start to turn a nice golden colour.

Add the thyme, pepper and sea salt and stir again. Add the white wine and let it sizzle, then add the chicken stock. Bring to the boil, then simmer for about 5 minutes.

Place the lettuce in a baking dish, cut side up, and pour over the liquid. Cover with foil and cook for about 20 minutes. The lettuce shouldn't be too soggy!

SERVES 4

Sesame seed zucchini

2 large zucchini

1 tablespoon olive oil

2 garlic cloves, finely sliced

1 teaspoon sesame seeds

sea salt and freshly ground pepper

Slice the zucchini into discs on the diagonal. Place in a bowl with the olive oil and garlic.

Heat a non-stick frying pan over medium heat. Add the zucchini and stir-fry for about 3 minutes. After 1–2 minutes, add the sesame seeds. Stir well.

Add the sea salt and pepper and stir for 1 minute. Remove from the pan and serve immediately.

SERVES 4

Stuffed zucchini flowers with ricotta chives and lemon zest

When it was last zucchini flower season, I was curious to see if I was happy with the flavour hit I got from a stuffed flower which was pan-fried instead of deep-fried. I was.

Rather than dipping the head of the zucchini in batter, I cooked each stem and flower in about 1 teaspoon of olive oil in a non-stick frying pan. I found the zucchini cooked well, and the flower's filling was warm inside and 'crusty' on the outside. A VERY tasty seasonal starter.

Don't be freaked out at the thought of 'stuffing' the petals. It's a bit tricky, just go easy… you don't have to do a hundred, around three per serve would be perfect.

250 g tub light ricotta cheese
1 tablespoon freshly snipped chives
zest of 1 lemon
sea salt and white pepper
6–8 zucchini flowers
4 tablespoons olive oil

Combine the ricotta, chives, lemon zest and sea salt and pepper.

Gently open the petals of the zucchini flowers and snap off the yellow stamen with your fingers.

Spoon in 1 teaspoon of the filling and twist the top.

Season the flower and stem with more sea salt and white pepper.

Heat 1 tablespoon of olive oil in a frying pan over medium heat. Pan-fry the zucchini flowers for 5–6 minutes, or until lightly golden. Add more olive oil as needed.

Before serving, cut off half the stem of the zucchini so you can stand them up on a serving tray.

SERVES 4

Roasted carrots with feta

3 carrots, cut on the diagonal
2 tablespoons olive oil
3 garlic cloves
sea salt and freshly ground pepper
½ teaspoon chilli flakes
100 g feta cheese
2 tablespoons chopped flat-leaf parsley

Preheat the oven to 200°C. Line a baking tray with baking paper.

Place the carrots in a bowl and pour in the olive oil and coat well. Add the sea salt, pepper and chilli flakes, then place on the baking tray.

Roast for about 25–30 minutes, or until nicely golden. Place the carrots in a dish and toss through the feta and parsley. Serve immediately.

SERVES 4

Pumpkin and cauliflower curry

½ butternut pumpkin, chopped into small cubes

250 g (1 cup) Greek yoghurt

1 knob of ginger, peeled and chopped

3 garlic cloves

1 teaspoon salt

1 teaspoon ground chilli powder

¼ teaspoon turmeric

1 tablespoon sunflower oil

1 teaspoon mustard seeds

3 bay leaves

5 cloves

1 teaspoon fenugreek seeds

1 long cinnamon stick

1 large onion, sliced

1 x 400 g tin tomatoes

1 bunch coriander

1 tablespoon cumin seeds

1 small handful mint

1 tablespoon dried or desiccated coconut

¼–½ teaspoon crushed chilli

1 teaspoon ground coriander

½ cauliflower

2 teaspoons garam masala

juice of 1 lemon

Combine the pumpkin, yoghurt, ginger, garlic, salt, chilli powder and turmeric in a bowl. Set aside.

Heat the sunflower oil in a non-stick frying pan over medium heat. Add the mustard seeds (careful, they will pop), bay leaves, cloves, fenugreek and cinnamon stick and cook for about 10–15 seconds.

Add the sliced onion and sauté until it turns golden brown.

Add the pumpkin mixture and stir through. Remove the bay leaves.

Process the tinned tomatoes, coriander (including the stems and leaves), cumin seeds, mint, coconut and onion mixture in a food processor until puréed.

Add the mixture to the frying pan along with the crushed chilli, ground coriander and the garam masala.

Add the cauliflower and 500 ml warm water. Simmer for about 40 minutes.

Just before serving, add a squeeze of the lemon juice, a little at a time, and stir through, being careful it doesn't curdle the yoghurt.

SERVES 4

I've generally been mean about desserts for this simple
reason: DESSERTS MAKE YOU FAT.

Ok, we've got that out of the way.

So, what if you're a sweet tooth and you really, really need
to have something après a meal to satisfy those cravings?
Cheesecake, crumble, tiramisu? Yep. But strap yourself in
for a few changes. Just close your eyes and *pretend* you're
eating the real calorie-laden sugary catastrophe and presto!

You can thank me later.

You'll notice that I've used coconut sugar instead of white
or brown sugar. You can buy coconut sugar at a place called
a HEALTH FOOD SHOP.

Affogato

Now here's MY idea of dessert. A sweet little scoop of the finest vanilla ice cream, served with a shot of the best espresso coffee. Yes, I know, ice cream, but it's just a little bit and I reckon that's cool, and it's not every night you have this right? RIGHT??

1 scoop per person of the best-quality vanilla ice cream you can afford

1 shot per person of espresso coffee

Prepare the espresso coffee in a shot glass.

In your favourite glass, place 1 small scoop of the ice cream. Place the glass on a small dish with the shot glass of coffee.

Serve with a long teaspoon and ask your guests to pour their own coffee over the ice cream.

SERVES 1

Chocolate-dipped strawberries

I haven't gone mad. Remember you are not to eat 30 strawberries yourself. About three will do the trick. Make sure they are uniform in shape. Serve with coffee.

3 large strawberries per person

150 g good-quality dark melting chocolate (70 per cent and above)

Prepare each strawberry by washing and drying but keep the leaves intact. Line a baking tray with baking paper.

Gently melt the chocolate over a bain-marie or in a small bowl in the microwave.

Dip each strawberry into the chocolate so that half is covered and place on the tray. Refrigerate until ready to serve.

To serve, use a nice platter and place each strawberry gently on the plate by using the leaf as a 'holder'.

SERVES 1

My cream of tiramisu

OK, cue the Italian music. Tiramisu is the queen of all Italian desserts and every mama and nonna has her own secret recipe that invariably includes loads of mascarpone cheese, sugar, eggs, grog and coffee-soaked savoiardi biscuits. Here's what I call a 'cream' of tiramisu. It has the flavours and textures of the real thing, but I kind of left out all the big fat mama bits. Remember the tip for desserts (and all meals)? Keep the serves small.

250 ml (1 cup) light cream

2 teaspoons coconut sugar

125 g (½ cup) light Greek yoghurt

125 ml (½ cup) espresso coffee (or 1 tablespoon instant coffee in ½ cup boiled water, cooled)

1 tablespoon Kahlua or other coffee-based liqueur

1 tablespoon best-quality cocoa powder

Whip the cream with the coconut sugar until it forms nice peaks. Gently fold through the yoghurt with a rubber spatula. Gently fold through the coffee, a little at a time. Gently fold through the liqueur.

Place the mixture in individual shot glasses and sift the cocoa powder over each glass.

Refrigerate for a few hours before serving.

SERVES 4

Lemony cheesecakes

Again sticking with the small-serving theory, these dollops of lemony cream will satisfy a sweet tooth at the end of a meal.

250 g tub light ricotta
250 g tub light cream cheese
juice of 1 lemon
zest of 1 lemon
4 teaspoons coconut sugar
2 teaspoons unsalted butter
100 g (1 cup) almond meal

Whip the ricotta, cream cheese, lemon juice, lemon zest and 2 teaspoons of the coconut sugar together until well combined.

Melt the butter and combine with the almond meal and the remaining coconut sugar.

Spoon some of the almond meal mix into the bottom of a cocktail glass. Then add some of the cheese mix. Refrigerate until ready to serve.

SERVES 4

Warm winter fruit salad

Citrus fruits are really at their best in the winter months in Australia. This fruit salad is juicy and zesty and if you want a grown-up kick, add a tablespoon of Cointreau.

1 orange, peeled and segmented
6 mandarins, peeled and segmented
1 grapefruit, peeled and segmented
185 ml (¾ cup) orange juice
1 tablespoon honey
1 tablespoon Cointreau or brandy
2 tablespoons flaked almonds

Place all the fruit in a serving bowl.

In a separate bowl, combine the juice, honey and liqueur. Pour over the fruit and combine well. Cover with plastic film and set aside.

When ready to serve, remove plastic wrap and sprinkle the flaked almonds over.

Serve with a bowl of yoghurt mixed with a little honey and some basil and mint leaves.

SERVES 4

Pears in red wine

Mum used to do this for dinner parties years ago, but I don't think it ever dates because it looks so gorgeous. Yes I've deboombah-ed the recipe but it still tastes lovely. Red-jewelled pears served with delicious yoghurt 'cream'. And the hint of basil is a refreshing twist.

400 ml red wine

3 teaspoons coconut sugar

1 cinnamon stick

4 pears

2 tablespoons Greek yoghurt

1 vanilla bean

2 basil leaves, finely shredded

(optional 1 teaspoon honey for your baby-ish guests)

Pour the wine into a saucepan and add the coconut sugar and cinnamon. Add the vanilla bean. Bring to a gentle boil, then turn down to a simmer. Add the pears and cook for about 1 hour.

Remove the pears and turn the heat up again on the syrup. Bubble for a few minutes, then remove from the heat. Remove the vanilla bean.

Blend the yoghurt with the basil (and honey if you must).

Serve each pear on a plate, drizzle with the syrup and serve with a little shot glass of yoghurt on the side.

SERVES 4

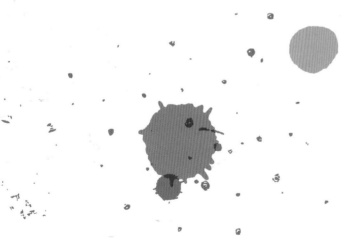

Rhubarb and strawberry crumble

4 stalks rhubarb, trimmed and cut into small pieces

1½ tablespoons coconut sugar

juice of 1 orange

170 g strawberries, trimmed

100 g (1 cup) almond meal

1 tablespoon flaked coconut

2 teaspoons butter

Preheat the oven to 180°C. Place the rhubarb, 2 teaspoons of the coconut sugar and orange juice in a small saucepan and bring to a gentle boil. Simmer for about 10 minutes, or until the rhubarb is soft. You may need to add a little water to make sure the rhubarb stays moist.

Add the strawberries and simmer a further 5 minutes.

Remove from the heat and pour the mixture into individual ramekins.

Combine the almond meal, coconut flakes, butter and the remaining coconut sugar and mix with your fingers to create the 'crumble'. Sprinkle a little mixture over each ramekin.

Bake for 20–25 minutes, or until bubbling and browned on top. Serve with a little dollop of Greek yoghurt if you like!

SERVES 4

Acknowledgements

Thank you to the fantastic team from Hardie Grant Books for encouraging this second book. Gordana Trifunovic, thank you for being such an easy-going editor and for leading the team with your positive (yet gently persuasive) manner and always putting everything in the 'sure, that can be done' basket for me. It made life so easy. Mark Roper, wow, again your stunning photos have flattered my often unglamourous dishes. Thanks for making the shoot such a pleasure. Thank you Trisha Garner, you've got the most fantastic eye for design; thank you for helping me create another book I am so proud of. Thanks again to Deb Kaloper for your calm manner, your sense of humour and your enormous styling talent. Michele Curtis and Andrea Geisler, thank you for whipping up the dishes for the book and thanks for asking me such great questions. Leesa O'Reilly, thanks again for filling this book with such beautiful pieces.

To Carrie, Celia, Richard and Annie Lou, thank you for being part of my dinner party in the book. One day I'll have a real one. Thanks again to Mum, Dad and Sandra for helping me get through an insane time combining cookbook-writing, work and taking care of five kids. Hirshy, thanks for your amazing support and friendship. And finally, to Rob, I promise I'll stop feeding you nine dishes a night to taste-test (at least until book number three).

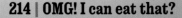

Index